PLAYING WITH WINE

(PUT A CORK IN IT)

GREG A. GONZALEZ

PLAYING WITH WINE

Laugh Line Publishing
1273 Regent Cir. Lincoln, CA 95648 U.S.A.

International Standard Book Number

978-0-9834255-3-3

Library of Congress Control Number 2011902464

Gonzalez, Greg A.

Playing With Wine

Produced in the United States of America

To everyone who has ever opened a bottle of wine,
tasted it and said something like
"mmmm this is good" without regard to the wine's
cost, pedigree, and rating that it received from someone
else's tongue.

CONTENTS

INTRODUCTION

For years we've heard that white wine goes with fish and red wine goes with meat. If one were to ask a fish it would say something like "what are we if not meat, chopped liver? Of course, if you removed our liver and chopped it up, then maybe we would be chopped liver or rather, liverless fish meat, but meat nonetheless."

Back to the wine question though. What if your fish is red like some salmon, or purple like ahi tuna, or even orange unlike orange roughy? Furthermore, what if you're colorblind? Shouldn't there be gray wines?

Then there's white meat to consider. Does it go with white wine? What if it's cooked in a red sauce? What then? Does guacamole pair with antifreeze since there aren't any green wines? The whole process of selecting a wine can be so confusing that one can have head pain before a single sip. It's no wonder that some people drink beer.

And there is also the big "what if." What if you're not hungry? Are you not allowed to have wine? What if you're getting ready to prepare your tax return and would like some wine while you whine? For that matter, there may not be any money left for food after doing your taxes, but a bit does remain for wine. The good part is that there really isn't any wine police yet and you get to decide what wine goes with what and when what wine goes with what and what the heck if the what that you want went with the what you don't want. Just pour a glass, relax, and enjoy.

WHY ANOTHER BOOK ON WINE

You can't have too many books like you can't have too much wine. Well, you can have too much wine, but that's a whole different set of books. Wine is a wonderful thing. It should be embraced, explored, and enjoyed. Try not to embrace it too firmly though or you may spill some on the carpet.

Most books on the subject aim to educate the reader on matters such as grape identification, history (insert yawn here), geography, culinary pairing, and how to taste. If you had strained peas as a baby and spit them out, then you've already learned how to taste. As far as grape identification goes, reading the label goes a long way in helping. The label on the wine bottle that is, as they don't put labels on grapes. It would be a real pain to have to peel the label off of each individual grape before snacking. Perhaps edible labels would be the answer, but we unferment. Or should that be we digress? The French, Germans, and Italians are beginning to show grape names on wine labels which previously just said something like Chateau le Grape de Whatever.

As far as the history of wine is concerned...when the bottle is empty the wine is history. Leave history to the historians. Don't leave it to the histerians. These are people that scream and jump up and down while pulling there hair out because history is no longer here. Geographically speaking, shouldn't we approach wine as some pro immigration activists approach illegal immigration? In other words, it matters not where one comes from or how he got here as long as he is here now. And since he is here, maybe he can pick some grapes.

The goal of this book is as simple as the goal of a fine wine; to be enjoyed. It is also the goal of a bad wine although not achieved nearly as often. Then we have the ten dollar wine whose goal is to be sold and possibly be enjoyed. Actually, the goal of this book may be closer to the that of the ten dollar wine, some of which are quite good.

In all fairness, this book does include geography, history, tasting, and lots of oenological vocabulary. However, there aren't any sulfites. The difference between *Playing With Wine* and the encyclopedia type wine books is that you won't be expecting a quiz at the end of each chapter.

CHAPTER ONE

PAIRING WINE WITH ANYTHING BUT FOOD

There are a few questions most of us ask about wine that aren't all that technical.

What does this wine go with?

How much does it cost?

How do you open the darn thing?

Why are the bottles so small?

What a wine goes with is the most common of these questions. Many wine books include a section dedicated to pairing wine with food. Many food books include a section dedicated to pairing food with wine. There are entire books on just pairing. Why does it even have to go with anything, other than a glass that is?

Suppose you're not hungry, have something better to do than eat, and would like some wine to go with that. What we've not seen in the wine world is the pairing of wine with activities. Here is one such guide that you can easily build on by trial and error. By the way D'Vine Wine from Texas goes best with forgiving errors. For that matter, after the trial in "trial and error" try a glass of Napa Valley's Justice wine. They offer a "Poetic Justice" red as well as a "Blind Justice" Cabernet. We assume that the Cabernet is also red, but then if justice really is blind then the color doesn't matter at all does it?

Anyways, here's the first installment of a nonfood wine pairing guide.

PAINTING: If the painting is creative in nature then you must have a bold red wine. A full-bodied Cabernet works well. One sip goes a long way between creative brush strokes. If you are painting a room then opt for a nicely chilled Pinot Grigio that isn't too expensive. It can refresh you and can also be used to clean the brushes.

AUTOMOBILE TRANSMISSION WORK: A dry and oaky Chardonnay such as one from Grgich Hills. Any red wine looks too much like transmission fluid and you wouldn't want to drink that by mistake. Although it's been said that the 1998 transmission fluid was not bad; the Detroit offering of course. Besides, by doing your own car repair you'll be able to afford this fine wine.

YOGA: A moderately priced Merlot such as Washington State's Columbia Crest Reserve. You want to stretch the muscles as you stretch your budget.

DOG BATHING: For large dogs, any red wine that has been corked (damaged by a mold in the cork thus ruining the wine). You'll be so frustrated with the dog that you won't notice the wine. It's going to get flea shampoo in it anyways. For small dogs, a glass of Sauvignon Blanc from the Loire Valley in France. The essence of cat pea in the wine will make for good irony.

CAT BATHING: A highly acetic Chardonnay that you can apply to the scratches. Room temperature would be best.

MOWING THE LAWN: Guenoc Sauvignon Blanc. It's inexpensive and has the scent of grass clippings, which could only be enhanced by your own lawn clippings. It is also quite refreshing and because of its low cost you won't mind fishing out little pieces of grass from the glass. Of course, if you're mowing where the dog does his business, then you may want to cover the glass.

MEETING PRESIDENT BARACK OBAMA: A tablespoon of Opus One. It is a blend of grapes and a collaboration between an American (Robert Mondavi) and a foreigner (Philippe de Rothschild). You get one tablespoon and the President gets the rest to squander on government programs.

INCOME TAXES: Your wine selection here should be something low in alcohol. You're going to need a lot of it, but don't give in to the pressure of trying an alcohol free wine. Why give the IRS the satisfaction? Perhaps a Riesling from Fetzer, Hogue, Mirassou, or Chateau Ste. Michelle. Be sure to keep it on the inexpensive side since you'll need the money for Uncle Sam. You know, by the way, that Uncle Sam is just going to use your tax dollars to serve fine German Rieslings at state dinners for foreigners that aren't even Americans. As they say in Washington DC, "you can't fight City Hall."

IRS AUDIT: If you just received the notice of an audit it's time to crack open some Hangtime Pinot Noir.

If things don't go your way send the auditor a bottle of Vampire White Zinfandel. You can also expect a call from them next year.

If the IRS throws the book at you, then send the auditor a bottle from France's Cote de Nuits. No, it isn't pronounced, "cut the nuts," you just feel that way.

MEETING FORMER PRESIDENT GEORGE W. BUSH: Kendall Jackson Meritage 2005. The label says "51% Cabernet Sauvignon, 46% Merlot and 3% Cabernet Franc." You know exactly what you're getting. It is unpretentious and modest. Of course, he won't be having any.

MEETING SECRETARY OF STATE HILLARY RODHAM CLINTON: Iron Horse Sparkling Brut served at room temperature. Hillary will provide the chill and the Iron Horse speaks for itself.

MEETING FORMER PRESIDENT BILL CLINTON: Yellow Tail Shiraz Reserve seems a good fit for the former president. Yes, it's Australian, but down under suits him just fine. It is a slick wine that's long on the palate with a strong finish. As sure as Syrah he'll schmooze your Shiraz off.

BURYING A DEAD GOLDFISH: For starters you wouldn't want to bury a live one. Burying isn't even the recommended departure method for a goldfish. There is no light at the end of the tunnel as there would be through some type of plumbing apparatus. Perhaps the Blue Fish Riesling from the Pfalz region of Germany would be an appropriate wine. It's supposedly clean and crisp with a sweet sendoff. Or should that read a sweet aftertaste for the afterlife?

WALKING ALONG THE BEACH: If it is a warm beach then BV Coastal Chardonnay out of a chilled boda bag. You aren't there for the wine as much as you are for the ocean, and if you happen to get a bit of sand in your wine it's no big deal. If the beach is cool then Robert Mondavi Merlot Coastal. Compared to wind, sand, rocks and shells it'll seem soft and smooth.

LISTENING TO RAP MUSIC: Any box wine will do, but drink the whole box to cleanse the palate before listening to the music.

PAYING BILLS: This task is usually performed in the morning and coffee is the beverage of mornings so a homemade coffee wine would be in order. There is such a thing and recipes can be found online.

HOLDING FOR CUSTOMER SERVICE: You'll likely be on hold for a long time so you don't want anything red. Your stomach will be brewing up enough tannin already. Chhabri from India comes to mind. It's a blend of Chardonnay, Thompson Seedless, and Ugni Blanc grapes. When the operator finally does come on the line, she can tell you more about this wine because she'll most likely be in India.

SWATTING MOSQUITOES: If the mosquitoes are out, then it's likely hot. A nicely chilled Moscato D'Asti would be perfect either by Fratelli for about $16 or Icardi for about $19, but not Barefoot Cellars or you might get stung. You can also use the empty bottle to take a swing at the little buggers.

POSTING BAIL: Aresti Chardonnay that has spent a little time in the cooler seems appropriate.

APPEARING AT TRIAL: None other than Alibi Merlot of course. It will go soft on you.

WATCHING RODEO: The Wild Horse Pinot Noir did win a silver medal at the 2009 San Francisco Wine Competition so it would be a match. Just don't let anyone see you drinking wine at a rodeo.

MOOSE HUNTING: The perfect wine for the end of a hunting trip would be 3 Blind Moose Cabernet. Be sure that you and your two hunting buddies don't have so much though that you become the 3 blind moose hunters.

POLO PLAYING: This pretentious sport calls for a fine sherry. Pour an odorous oloroso for the appaloosas.

WAITING AT THE BUS STATION: A bottle of Bolla Valpolicella goes best here. It is very inexpensive. If you had any money, you wouldn't be at a bus station. Be sure to keep it in a paper bag. When a passing hobo asks for a drink of what's in the bag you just tell him that it's Valpolicella and he'll think you're an undercover police officer.

OPRAH WINFREY: For appearing on her show to sell some books it has to be Veuve Clicquot La Grande Dame. She'll know what it is and will appreciate the reference. Too bad her daytime show isn't on anymore.

HOUSE HUNTING: By house hunting we mean searching online. If shopping in a warm climate then go with Big House White. If shopping in a cooler climate have the Big House Red. If shopping in the San Francisco Bay Area then, by all means, have the Big House Pink.

PACKING TO MOVE: A box wine, of course. The Almaden Blush in a box fits the bill perfectly here. In packing you inevitably will come across some old clothes and works of art sure to make you blush from the embarrassment of having had so little taste back then.

UNPACKING AFTER MOVING: There are many American wines with chateau in the name and far more French wines from "le chateau such and such" to "chateau de whatnot." Just look at a list and pick one. Don't pick an expensive wine, however, since you'll be drinking it out of the bottle or an old coffee can because you don't know where the stemware is.

BREAKING A MIRROR: Of course, many chards come to mind; or would that be shards. How about the 2006 Chateau Giscours Margaux? It should be spectacular in 7 years after your bad luck runs out.

HAVING YOUR CAR REPAIRED: If it's a German car then a glass of Dr. Loosen Riesling would be good, especially if you have tight lug nuts.

For a Japanese car you would quickly think that Saki would be recommended, but that would be stereotypical and too easy a selection. Hmmm, is using stereo and Japanese in the same sentence also stereotypical? Better to go with something from Pacific Rim Winery.

For an American car you'll have to go with something from a unionized winery, perhaps Gallo. Expect to pay more for it and get less quality.

If you have a Yugo then get a box wine because you'll be there for a long time.

WATCHING NETWORK NEWS: From the Umbria region of Italy comes Opinioni. The mainstream media seems to prefer Europe to the United States. They'll not give you news as much as their opinion and you should take umbrage.

READING DANTE'S DIVINE COMEDY: What else but the 7 Deadly Zins Zinfandel would go with this activity?

SMOKING A CIGAR: Since this isn't a book about brandy, you'll have to settle for a glass of Churchill Cellars Pinot Noir.

ON THE RUN FROM THE LAW: How about some Gewurztraminer from Jekel. Get it? Jekel and Hide. Just like all wines aren't good, all jokes aren't either.

WATCHING A MOVIE: Francis Ford Coppola Presents Chardonnay would be perfect unless you're watching a film noir. In this case go for the Pinot.

CALLING AN EXTERMINATOR: Chateau LaGrande Roche goes for about $30 to $40 a bottle, but you can consider it part of the cost of extermination. Save half of this Cabernet because two treatments are usually required.

SHOPPING FOR A DREAM CAR: Testarossa offers a Syrah with a lot of horsepower. Of course, if this isn't in your budget then you can drive a glass of Red Truck.

WATCHING A FIRE: Sea Smoke Pinot Noir from Santa Barbara County is just the wine to cool the embers.

READING SHAKESPEARE: Consider taking in the words of the bard with a glass of Sonnet Pinot Noir. Limit thyself to one glass or thou willeth be slurring thy words.

GOING BOATING: Any wine that isn't too heavy should be fine for such an activity. Be sure to purchase it "on sail."

DECIDING WHETHER TO GO TO THE GYM OR FOSTER'S FREEZE: This calls for a small glass of Paraduxx. These wines are blends, but then so are milk shakes.

WATCHING RERUNS OF COLUMBO: Anything that you can find from Palumbo Family Vineyards will work. I know it's not a particularly clever selection, but hey, you're the one watching a TV show from the 70's; how picky can you be?

LISTENING TO PETER PAUL AND MARY FROM THE 1960s: If you turn down the treble and turn up the bass then some Merlot from Peter Paul Wines will resonate since you will have eliminated most of Mary. Peter Paul also works well for reading some of the New Testament.

BUILDING A MANGER: While we're on the subject of the Bible, there's a winery in Berkeley, California called Donkey and Goat, which would be perfect for such an activity.

WAITING FOR THE APOCALYPSE: A generous glass of Merlot from Godwin in the Alexander Valley of Sonoma County seems appropriate. Of course, there are those who would prefer some Chardonnay from Diablo Creek. You should be warned though that it could be a little heavy on the sulfites.

CROSSING THE U. S. BORDER ILLEGALLY: The Migration Pinot Noir made by Duckhorn would be perfect. Be sure to carry a lot of water as well. You can use the water to cleanse the palate or to stay alive. If you could slightly chill the Pinot in the 115 degree desert, that would be nice as well. Don't forget to pack some paté de foie gras if available.

WATCHING RERUNS OF THE GOLDEN GIRLS: A nicely aged bottle of Cabernet Sauvignon from Geezer Peak would be just perfect. Make that Geyser Peak.

WATCHING MSNBC: This cable news channel demands a respectable selection, but has no audience so any wine will do. You really shouldn't drink alone.

WATCHING FOX NEWS: The Foxen Red Blend table wine (you can call it a red state table wine) is fairly priced and well balanced.

READING EMILY DICKINSON: Poet's Leap from Columbia Valley in Washington has a very highly regarded Riesling, which you could chill for a reading. If by chance you happen to be reading Robert Frost, then just chill it a little bit more.

READING OTHER POETRY: Byron's Pinot Noir would be a classic selection. It is said to walk in beauty…soft like candlelight and not too overpowering.

FISHING ON THE COAST: From New York hails Salmon Run Chardonnay. It's inexpensive and not highly rated. After scooping the innards out of a large fish what does it matter?

APPLYING FOR SOCIAL SECURITY RETIREMENT: If there is any left, opt for a reserve Chardonnay from Ponzi. A reserve may be all that remains in Social Security

FRATERNITY GATHERING: Of course, only those frat brothers of legal drinking age are invited and can share a bottle of Napa Valley's Screw Kappa Napa. If they made an Italian brandy then you could possibly have Phi Beta Kappas sharing Screw Kappa Napa Grappa.

SORORITY GATHERING: A selection from Three Sisters Vineyards out of Lumpkin County Georgia could very well be pleasing. For a larger sorority though, go with one of the rose' wines from Four Sisters Winery in Belvidere, New Jersey.

DUCK HUNTING: No hunter is complete without his Decoy red wine from Napa Valley. The higher end hunters would prefer Duckhorn Merlots, which are generally highly rated. Give it a quack.

DANCING: Take a glass of Malbec from Hey Mambo onto the floor and give it a whirl. If you're not a great dancer try the Chardonnay by Dancing Bull.

VISITING AN ART MUSEUM: Viewing the Mona Lisa calls for a Brunello di Montalcino also by Davinci although not the same one I'm pretty sure. Both are works of art. Don't get any on the canvas.

ATTENDING THE OPERA: Tosca makes a Pinot Grigio that was well received by critics. Coincidentally, Giacomo Puccini produced a Tosca that was well received by critics. The Tosca is worth comparing to the Pinot Grigio by Placido. Both of these are Italian wines. The Zinfandel by Giuseppe is worth looking at if you prefer red wine. It's not so bohemian, or rather "La Boheme."

ATTENDING A LOLLAPALOOZA CONCERT: A glass of Red Blend from Italy's La Palazzola could match the hoopla from Lollapalooza.

TENDING TO DIAPER RASH: A little Sauvignon Blanc from Babich out of New Zealand will calm your worries and it may even help if you dab a bit on the baby's "down under."

GETTING A TATTOO: A Malbec with its dark color makes a great substitute for ink in case the artist runs out. Try a glass by Infinitus. Oh, and guess how long you'll have that mark on your skin.

TATTOO REMOVAL: If you're seeing a qualified professional to correct a bodily typo then enjoy some Prosecco by La Marca. With luck the mark will be gone by the time your glass is dry.

RUNNING A POLITICAL CAMPAIGN: What else but some Sangiovese by Machiavelli would be appropriate? A decent wine for a sometimes indecent proposal.

PLAYING WITH DOLLS: If your name is Ken and you're of legal drinking age, then you shouldn't be playing with dolls in the first place. If you must and have $50 or so try Brunello by Barbi. Brunello is what the locals in Tuscany call Sangiovese. We have a pretty good idea what Ken's locals call him.

WORKING IN THE GARDEN: Turning Leaf has a Pinot Grigio than can cool you off a bit after raking. If you buy the three liter box then you can sprinkle some on the ground to keep the dust down.

GETTING STUNG BY A SCORPION: If you are allergic, call 911, relax, and pour a glass of Cristal Champagne by Louis Roederer. Yes, it's very expensive, but it may be your last. If you survive, celebrate with another glass.

FAMILY DISCUSSIONS: Loosen up, be honest, don't hold back, and pass around some Frank Family Cabernet. Hopefully, your family is small. This will leave more wine for you.

GOING TO THE AIRPORT: If the pilots haven't finished it all, try some Pinot Noir by Flying Goat Cellars out of California's Central Coast. They make several Pinots so book the round trip.

READING A CHEAP NOVEL: It may be an inexpensive remark, or rather; a cheap shot, but Harlequin Syrah from Washington may be a good accompaniment to stories of intrigue, passion, and betrayal.

PICKING MUSHROOMS: Don't try this if you don't know Shiitake from Shinola. These days younger folk don't know Shinola from granola. Take a bottle of Forest Glen's Shiraz along. Put some fun in the fungus.

DECISION MAKING: Trying to decide whether to spend the holidays with the in-laws or in Hawaii? This is a conundrum for which there is Conundrum. Actually, in some cases it may be a "no brainer." If you happen to live in Hawaii then you're probably stuck with the in-laws visiting you.

IMPRESSING A CLIENT: If it's a big deal and the client knows wine well, then a Cabernet from Harlan Estate must be your selection. This isn't funny, nor is it meant to be. On the other hand, if you were to break the cork, splash wine on the client's $300 white shirt, lose the deal and subsequently your job, it could be funny. At least to someone else it could be.

WATCHING A STEEPLECHASE EVENT: The Chardonnay by Leaping Horse will work if it's warm out. The Shiraz works better on cool days. If such events are too elitist for your taste, then open up a bottle of Leaping Lizard Chard and make your own race. Although, how you get a lizard to let you ride it and jump is beyond me.

FORTUNE TELLING: Harbinger out of Napa Valley has a Merlot you could enjoy while reading palms. It doesn't cost a fortune either, but then you knew that.

CELL PHONE RINGING AT A MOVIE: Spring for some Rudd Cabernet Sauvignon to share with those around you. It's expensive and it serves you right.

CALLING A PLUMBER: It's time to pay the piper. Celebrate that your toilet now flushes with a glass of Piper Heidsieck Champagne. Ask the plumber to wash his hands first.

JUST SITTING THERE WITH NOTHING TO DO: We don't mean on the toilet that you just got fixed, but rather just sitting there. Bordeaux of course! If this happens a lot then have the Bordeaux Altime.

TRYING ON SHOES: If it fits try the Alsace region's Schoffit Riesling. It wears well.

PREPARING A WILL: Jargon Pinot Noir can ease the legalese used at times such as these. By the way, who ever says bequeath unless they're writing a will? Picture a parent preparing their last will and testament while the kids are yelling in the background. "Be quiet. Can't you see I'm bequeathing?"

BEHAVING ASININE WITH LAW ENFORCEMENT: One of Tuscany's finest is what you'll face. Poliziano Asinone is the best wine for such an occasion, but they'll probably take it away from you. It is, by the way, a Vino Nobile di Montepulciano D. O. C. G. I think that's like New York's finest for Italian wines.

DRINKING ALONE: You really shouldn't, but if you must, try some Hermitage from France's Northern Rhone region, just don't overdo it. Remember, wine goes best with people.

BEING ROBBED: Bordeaux' Chateau Dassault from St. Emilion fits the crime. Don't buy it in a restaurant though or you will have been taken twice.

MAKING PLANS WITHOUT CHECKING FIRST: Bring home a bottle of Mad Housewife Chardonnay and everything will be just fine. It's really cheap at only about seven bucks. Be sure to leave the price tag on it. She'll know that you are really sincere and would never again make such a mistake.

MAKING UP FOR BUYING THE CHEAP WINE IN THE PREVIOUS SUGGESTION: Nothing less than Perrier Jouet Fleur de Champagne will get you out of this mess. If you buy the gift pack that they offer for about $120 then she may share some with you.

MAKING UP FOR OVERSPENDING ON THE CHAMPAGNE: It's time to pretend that you're thoughtful and go European. A bottle of Germany's Schweinhardt Scheurebe Spatlese should smooth things over. A word of caution, however. Don't call it "Sure baby schweinhund." It's Schweinhardt Scheurebe.

BLIND DATE: Please choose anything but Ugly Duckling Chardonnay.

A GIFT FOR AN AEROBICS INSTRUCTOR: Any selection by Fat Bastard out of France would be the obvious choice.

GIFT FOR YOUR PREGNANT WIFE: Treat her to a bottle of Bubbly by Barefoot Cellars, but do so during the first trimester only.

DEATH OF GLOBAL WARMING THEORY: Au Bon Climat for everyone. Al Gore may say that the Pinot Noir goes down a little hot, but this is just a normal climatic windbag effect.

GETTING YOUR DOG FROM THE KENNEL: Cellar No. 8 Cabernet is cheap, not too bad and what the hell does a resentful dog know about wine anyway?

FOR ANY BIRTHDAY OVER THE LEGAL DRINKING AGE: Marie Antoinette may have let them eat cake. Sipping Cakebread is a much better option.

CELEBRATING WEIGHT LOSS: This calls for a full-bodied Petite Sirah. Spend a little extra to get a good one because you deserve it. When they say that it should be served with rich food they aren't referring to a whole chocolate cake. Just thought that you should know.

STARTING A DIET: The Merlot by Little Black Dress is a good choice if you're just starting a diet. The Primitivo out of Puglia, Italy by Layer Cake Wines is a bit premature at this time. Save it until you reach your goal.

BACHELOR PARTY: You're tempted to serve some of Stag's Leap many fine Cabernets, but they will be wasted on most of the attendees so stick with beer. If you insist on wine, however, go with the Marilyn Merlot paired up with either Rodney Strong or Rex Goliath.

BRIDAL SHOWER: The temptation here is to serve something elegant befitting the occasion such as Ferrari-Carano Chardonnay. This is especially true if your name is Ferrari and you're marrying a Carano. The same applies to Murphy-Goode or even Kendall-Jackson, but what's the likelihood? Play it safe and go with the Chardonnay by Virgin Vines.

BIRD WATCHING: There are many wines with birds on the label. It is not known why since birds don't drink wine. Select one that is light and crisp such as Chile's Anakena Sauvignon Blanc. Note, however, that if you start seeing two headed ducks such as on Anakena's label then try something lighter.

CLEANING UP THE BEACH: Kosta Browne Pinot Noir is the obvious choice here. Of course, if you're cleaning up after an oil spill then opt for the Black Swan Chardonnay.

WATCHING FLINTSTONES RERUNS: Transport yourself to "Bedrock" with a bottle of The Bedrock Heirloom from Sonoma County. One of the oldest vineyards in California produces this blend of Zinfandel, Carignan, and a cast of many other characters. One must wonder if the label describes the wine as tasting like "fruity pebbles."

STANDING OVATION: A nice round of Two Hands Shiraz from Australia will bring the performance to a nice close. The sound of one hand clapping is due to the other holding a glass of wine and not wanting to spill.

FINISHING A BOOK: If it's the first one that you've written then celebrate with a bit of cautious optimism and a bottle of Louis Roederer Brut Premier at about $45. When it sells you can graduate to Dom Perignon.

If you've just finished reading a book then go with the everyday wine of your choice.

TAKING MEDICATION: For starters the medicine bottles should be clearly marked as to whether they go best with white wine or red wine. Antibiotics could possibly go with a sparkling wine. Blush wines pair up nicely with conditions of the skin. You'd better check with your doctor first though.

On a side note, shouldn't the medicine bottles also be so easy to open that even a child could do it?

CHAPTER TWO

A MATTER OF TASTE

There is nothing more personal than taste. Maybe not even hygiene. Person A can eat a dab of a fine French Brie and want to share the pleasurable experience of that taste with person B, but can't. At least not completely. Everyone's taste is different. The difference may be slight or great. Person B could have a diminished sense of smell due to genetics or maybe had some taste buds shot off in battle, be it the Middle East or the East of Los Angeles. Regardless, that Brie might just wind up tasting to person B like some creamy bacterial fungus paste with the essence of athlete's foot. Oh, you mean it's supposed to taste like that? The point is that tasting wine is as subjective as something gets.

Many of us have seen wine tasting either at a winery, in the movies, or on television. The process is usually performed with the most serious of faces. Picture the face of a surgeon applying scalpel to lung tissue, or submitting your tax return to an IRS agent, or awaiting the approval of your credit card by that little plastic machine at a store. Relax, it won't hurt a bit.

Here is a little half serious introduction to get you on your tasting way. The good news is that no matter what, you don't have to like it.

AERATION (A fancy way of saying breathe, or "someone open a window.")

Of course the wine must breathe prior to tasting. This can be accomplished a variety of ways. The traditional method of removing the cork thus allowing air to enter the bottle is still the necessary first step in the process. Unscrewing the cap has joined uncorking as a means of aeration. Drilling holes in the sides of the bottle hasn't shown to work very well and busting off the top of the bottle against a countertop went out with the 1880's and is now only advisable if you have good health insurance. Of course, if you happen to be in the middle of the Kalahari Desert with a bottle of Beaujolais and no corkscrew, the last method would be acceptable. Good luck finding a countertop in the middle of the desert though.

Another traditional step in allowing a wine to breathe is to get it out of the bottle. The process of pouring the wine into another container is called decanting. There are special containers for holding wine that has been decanted. They are called, believe it or not, decanters. Of course, in you want to serve the wine to your guests directly from the bottle you could empty it into another vessel and then funnel it back into the wine bottle for pouring. It is very important to note here not to use the same funnel with which you add gasoline to the lawn mower. You may be able to get away with it if you're pouring a $3.99 selection purchased at some discount outlet, but for the most part, not.

These days many have taken to using wine aerators. Such devices which either attach to the bottle or through which wine is poured allows the wine to, so they say, be instantly aerated. Call me old fashioned, but I prefer to give my wines "mouth to mouth." Even if you simply pour a glass of wine and allow it to sit in between sips you'll notice how the flavor changes as time elapses. Breathing may be overrated for the majority of wines, as they are ready to enjoy off the rack. Experiment with this and decide for yourself.

STEMWARE (This was once called glasses, goblets, and cups.)

In 1982, the author purchased a bottle of 1971 Sonoma County something or other red wine. At the time it was the oldest bottle he'd seen. Wouldn't it be cool to drink this right out of the bottle? As it turns out the experience was nothing special and a straw probably wouldn't have helped either. That wine would have been best enjoyed sipped from a proper glass.

Some will say that it matters not what you drink out of and others will say that it matters some. Then there are those whom would rather forego tasting a Lafite than sip it from a Viognier glass. All you need to do is drink a sampling of the same wine from a coffee cup, a wine glass, a paper cup, the dog's dish, and a landscaper's boot. You'll immediately know that wine glasses are best. That is not to say that you must spend $25 per glass to enjoy wine.

Crystal glasses, either colored or clear, look great, but alter the view of the wine. They are best left for display. Of course, if you insist that these twenty four per cent lead hand cut Swarovski works of art were made for using, then you can always serve chocolate milk to the children in these on special occasions. Wine tasting is an area where simple elegance works best. Many will agree that the glasses by Riedel are the best for wine. Riedel has a different shaped glass for what seems like every varietal in existence and then some. They are clear smooth glass with thin lips for the most part and range in size from a small tulip shaped Riesling glass to what could almost past for a fishbowl in the way of a Pinot Noir glass. A bigger bowl is generally better than small. It allows for a better view and one can more safely swirl the wine on a white rug with one of these. They are expensive, but have been found in thrift shops for a mere 99 cents. It's funny though, those 99-cent stores don't carry them. Also, be sure to buy extra glasses, because they do break. Some of these fragile vessels have been known to break from merely the attitude of a first growth Bordeaux and others have broken from just banging them on a cast iron sink during washing.

SPIT HAPPENS (Some baby coined this phrase, we believe, and it happens in wine tasting as well.)

The wine is poured but not to the rim and if you were expecting a head on it you'd be disappointed. Usually it's poured about one third full. This helps protect the carpet. Grab the glass by the stem and tilt it on its axis to get a better look at the clarity and color. This is hardly essential to enjoying wine and to some it's downright foolish. To others it adds to an already enjoyable experience. Well, it's not that enjoyable yet since you've not tasted anything.

Before tasting, stick your nose deep down into the bowl of the glass and take a few sniffs. Don't take one big long sniff for danger of drowning. Try it again. There are more scents used in describing wine than a dog can find in a public park. You'll hear about citrus, grass, vanilla, cinnamon, berries, stones, leather, smoke, tobacco, and occasionally cat pea. As long as it isn't dog pea, then you're probably ok. There may even be times where you can't tell if that being described is wine or a rodeo.

Taste the wine. Take in a generous amount. Slurping is not only allowed, it is encouraged. Slosh it around in your mouth to make contact with all areas of taste. It is not necessary to repeat these steps for the entire evening. You will no doubt irritate others and may get slapped. After the slurp and slosh, if you care to, identify the various items that you taste. These can vary from cassis, whatever that is, to lychees and in the case of some Rieslings, Interstate 5 comes through. The one item according to wine circles that you should not taste is grapes. How silly is that? Imagine ordering a beer and asking that it not taste like beer. "Waiter, I think I'll order the steak au poivre and please be sure that it tastes like fish."

The professional wine tasters at this point would proceed to spit the wine out into a bucket. I could understand this if it was my mother's cooking that was being tasted, but not good wine. Of course, if one tastes many wines at a time the need for objectivity and sobriety necessitate spitting. As long as they hit the bucket and not your shoes, it's probably all right. If you aren't at a snooty tasting event, repeat the above steps without spitting one or two more times and then proceed to just enjoy the wine for the gift from God that it is.

CHAPTER THREE

MEET THE GRAPES

You no doubt have noticed that red wine is not really red and white wine isn't white. Come to think of it, black people aren't black, brown people aren't brown, yellow people certainly aren't yellow, and white people aren't white either. Whites don't even remotely resemble white wine. It's all a big gray area. If anything, people look more like bread than wine. And what goes better with wine than bread? Oh yeah, cheese. People don't resemble cheese either unless you're talking about some fans of the Green Bay Packers with their cheese hats. Better than bread or cheese with wine are people. Now don't go taking a bite out of Uncle Charlie to pair up with your Pinot Noir. You know what we mean

According to The Wine Guide by Williams-Sonoma, wine was drunk about 4000 B.C. in the Middle East. If there was ever a place that could use some wine today. In the beginning was the word and the word was good. A good while thereafter was the wine and the wine was not so good. This may have been due to storage in inferior oak barrels or at above 56 degrees Fahrenheit, or perhaps the first batch of wine was just a puddle of funky old grape juice laying on the side of the road in a wooden vessel waiting for a thirsty passerby. There wasn't any water around and being in the Middle East you probably wouldn't want to drink the water anyways. This rotten grape juice would have to do. The aroma was not one of citrus, melons, and wildflowers on a fresh spring day. It would have been more like mushrooms, camels, and perspiration in the middle of August. Regardless, it was liquid from fruit and the effect wasn't bad either.

It is with wine that most special occasions are celebrated. Champagne is served at New Years, weddings, and at Champagne brunches. Sometimes sparkling wine is substituted for Champagne. Religious ceremonies include wine. Jesus Christ shared wine with the apostles. It is not a drop of Budweiser that the Mohel (Rabbi) places in a child's mouth at a bris, but rather wine. At least, that's how it was done in an episode of M*A*S*H years ago. Then again, in such a situation brandy might be preferred, but that's just me. Hopefully, you'll forgive my lack of Jewishness.

At its simplest wine is a wonderful thing. At its most complex wine is a wonderful thing. Complexity is a descriptive term frequently used to describe wine. It concerns a wine's balance with regard to aromas and flavors. There used to be only two terms to describe a wine; yummy or yucky. As with most things evolution brings about an expansion of ideas or shall we say complexity. Yummy and yucky were soon followed by terms such as "puke that is," "what a bunch of crap," and "an elegant bouquet with the essence of daffodils and wildebeest followed by a Wagnerian opera-like finish." Regardless of the words the enjoyment of wine is one of life's greatest pleasures. It is best enjoyed simply and often.

It all begins with the grapes. Of course, the question is begged. Which came first the grape or the seed? The answer may or may not be known. Perhaps a chicken passed a seed. Back to the grapes. A wine novice might think that there are two kinds of grapes, red and white. Those more educated know that there are also pink grapes and grapes with bubbles in them. There are even pink grapes with bubbles in them. These are called "Cold Duck" grapes and dropped out of fashion at about the same time that bell-bottomed pants did.

In addition to red, white, sparkling, and pink wines (rosé), there are fortified wines. No, this is not a wine that causes one to emit odorous fumes. You're thinking of fartified. One could think that these five varieties of wine grapes run the gamut, but nothing could be farther from the truth. It's not like the former Soviet Union where you had two styles of shoes, right and left.

Most wine grapes come from a single species of grape, Vitis Vinifera. Depending on whom you ask, there are anywhere from 5000 to 10000 different grape varietals throughout the world within this species. Thompson Seedless, Red Flame, Ruby Seedless, and Autumn Royal are table grapes from another Vitis altogether. There's Vitis Labrusca, Vitis Riparia, Vitis Rotundifolia, Vitis Mustangensis and others. There are even hybrid grape species like the Vitis Toyota Prius. Of course, you didn't buy this book to become an ampelographer or to brush up on your Latin so I'll spare you any more Vitis. By the way, an ampelographer is a botanist that identifies grape vines. Either that or something that you plug your electric guitar into so as to make it louder. And someone that studies Latin is called a Latino.

The most widely planted wine grape in the world is something called Airen. It comes from Spain. More people know Air Jordan than know Airen. There is also Auxerrois, not to be confused with Axl Rose from Guns N' Roses. Auxerrois is a fairly common French wine grape. What about Bourboulenc? Imagine borrowing a bottle of bourboulenc bubbly from a buddy named Bubba. Have you ever heard of Garganega? It's a northern Italian wine grape. Picture yourself gorging on garbanzos and Gorgonzola with a gargantuan glass of Garganega, in a gondola near Genoa.

What about Mauzac from the Languedoc-Roussillon used to make Cremant de Limoux? Then there is the Greek grape called Moscofilero. "Hand me the moscofilero so that I can swat this bug." Muller-Thurgau is the most widely planted grape in Germany and, if not mistaken, an Amish furniture manufacturing company in Pennsylvania. I've read that Palomino is a major grape of Sherry. If that's what she calls her grapes I wonder what she calls her horse. Scuppernong is a grape native to the southeastern United States. Feed enough of these to your dog and be prepared to bring out the pooper scoopernong.

Alicante Bouschet is a red wine grape widely planted in California during prohibition. Growers would transport to the east coast a bunch of Bouschet during this alleged dry period in our history. Pardon the corniness of the next line. Do you suppose that all of the wines during prohibition were dry? Bastardo is the Portuguese grape that only has a mother. Then there's Blaufrankisch. Isn't that one of the gifts that the wise men brought to Jesus? Gold, myrrh and Blaufrankisch? That must have been frankincense since Jesus would have been too young for wine at the time.

Carignan is either a grape used for blending or some sort of sweater. In Chile some wines labeled as Merlot include the grape Carmanere. The Chilean wine police have been overheard saying "come here comrade; I am commandeering your Carmanere." Perhaps not. The Italian grape Tazzelenghe translates to tongue cutting. Fitting, given the mouthful word that it is. Finally, at least for now, there's Vaccarese from France commonly used in the making of Chateauneuf-du-Pape. This many wine grapes are enough to give the reader a case of vaccarese veins for which you'll need a jar of Cremant de Limoux. It can be overwhelming especially since we've just scratched the surface.

The key to appreciating and enjoying wine is to sip and not chug. Take some time to explore one type of wine or style before moving on to the next. Many wine lovers begin their journey through the vineyards with an easier drinking white wine such as a Riesling before tangling with a "titannic" Cabernet Sauvignon or getting mauled by a Malbec.

CLASSIC GRAPES

The classic grape designation comes from well, the same place that "Classic Rock" comes from. A lot of people from a lot of places liked it a lot when it came out and still do. Remember this goes back thousands of years; like Keith Richards. Depending on whom you ask there may be anywhere from six classic grape varieties to as many as fourteenish. Some are indeed classic whereas, others are just important works. Classic grapes are also referred to as "Noble Grapes." The most important grape of all has always been the one presently in your glass.

CLASSIC WHITE GRAPES

CHARDONNAY (You bet it is ubiquitous)

This grape does well everywhere and is thus planted everywhere. The vines produce a good yield and do well in varied climates. Right now there is probably some penguin crushing Chardonnay grapes for the next release of Chateau du Antarctica. Okay, so it's not really planted everywhere, but it is more ubiquitous than any other varietal.

The Chardonnay grape originally is from Burgundy in France and is a major grape of Champagne. Burgundy to wine novices is a cheap red jug wine and Chablis is a cheap white jug wine. Actually, white Burgundies are wines made from Chardonnay grapes as are Chablis'. They are some of the most expensive and yummy wines in the world. The bottles, of course, won't likely say Chardonnay on the label. Such is true for most, but not all French wines. It is presumed, for the most part, that if you buy a wine from say Cote D'Or, that you know you're buying Chardonnay. The same goes for Maconnais, Mersault, Cote' Chalonnaise, Pouilly-Fuisse, and Puligny-Montrachet, but not Chaise Lounge'. In the latter case you're buying some sort of sofa.

In California, the bottles are labeled showing the grape variety. If it says Chardonnay, then that's the grape used. This does not mean that it won't taste like lumber soaked in acid with a side of butter though.

Many California Chardonnays are not so good. Finding a good inexpensive "Chard" as some would say, takes some work and research. The "you get what you pay for" rule is usually, but not always, a good one to follow. A five-dollar Chardonnay will not likely be as satisfying as say a thirty dollar Rombauer Chard from California. Then again, you never know.

Great Chardonnays come from France, California, Australia, New Zealand, Italy, Eastern Europe, South America, South Africa and maybe even South Philly. As many as there are great Chardonnays, though, there are indeed crappy ones.

The flavors of Chardonnay include butter, oak, vanilla, citrus, apples, minerals, acid, and more. It really depends on the individual grapes and what was done to them. Now it doesn't necessarily work in reverse. Try licking a cube of butter to see if it tastes like Chardonnay and you'll see what I mean. This wine is better with food than by itself, but then that always depends on the person and the Chardonnay.

SAUVIGNON BLANC (Not only for when you don't want anymore Chardonnay)

This grape is also a transplant from France, but rather the Bordeaux region as opposed to Burgundy. It produces, like Chardonnay, a dry wine unless it is blended with other grapes in the making of dessert wines such as Sauterne. Where Chards can be described as powerful locomotives, Sauvignon Blancs would be more like bullet trains. These wines tend to be smoother, fresher and not as harsh. Citrus and grassy are terms commonly used in describing Sauvignon Blancs.

New Zealand is becoming more and more popular in the wine world due to the excellent Sauvignon Blancs originating there. You may have noticed some wines labeled Fume' Blanc. Fume' is a Sauvignon Blanc with a marketing department. The name, it is said, was invented by the American wine legend Robert Mondavi to help sell the wine. In the Loire region of France Blanc Fume' is synonymous with Sauvignon Blanc. So if Fume' Blanc is Blanc Fume' then Sauvignon Blanc could be called Blanc Sauvignon. Digress I.

As the cool people say "Chard" in referring to Chardonnay, some also say "Sauv Blanc" instead of enunciating the entire Sauvignon Blanc. Its sheer laziness wrapped up in chic I tell ya. People will try to save syllables wherever they can. For example we have a dog whose name is Kujo. It's a name that's two syllables long and we call him Kooj for short. How lazy we Americans have gotten. Especially the younger folks who've practically reduced the Standard General American language to one continuous mumbled syllable that only they can understand. It must go with that typing with thumbs only. This laziness may be the reason they're eliminating corks from wine bottles and replacing them with screw caps, but who's to say?

Sauvignon Blanc has been described as the best California food wine due to its versatility. Others think that it is one of the best foods period. Generally, they aren't fermented in oak barrels, as are the Chards, but there are many exceptions.

RIESLING (Grape often used as a launching pad)

Many newcomers to wine begin with Rieslings. This wine is generally described as lighter, sweeter, and more refreshing than others. Of course, many Rieslings are also dry. The grape's roots are in Germany where the best Rieslings come from. Many of the finest vines grow on the steep slate vineyards along the Mosel River. If you've ever licked a piece of slate and had a fine Riesling from the Mosel or Rhine Valleys you could notice some similarities. Harvesting on these steep slopes, is accomplished using trained goats without inner ear problems, although, we could be mistaken. The Alsace region of France (near the German region of Germany) is also known for producing fine Rieslings as are vineyards in Australia, New Zealand and of course, California.

Just as in the home decorating television shows, fruity and floral are terms commonly used when referring to Riesling. Some lower priced Rieslings from Germany and elsewhere do resemble soda pop without the fizz and oenophiles typically view this as a negative. A little flat pop never hurt anybody. In keeping with the train analogy mentioned earlier, a Riesling would be an electric commuter light rail. The milder, less expensive mass produced wines of this variety are hardly noticed. The fines ones, on the other hand, are quite elegant.

CLASSIC RED GRAPES

PINOT NOIR (So cool that the T is silent)

Burgundy is synonymous with Pinot Noir. We're referring to Burgundy the place in France not burgundy the swill put out by Ernest and Julio Gallo. Some would say that this is harsh. This may be, but not as harsh as the Gallo. In fact, it's probably best served in the gallows so that the condemned won't mind going so much.

Pinot Noir tends to be fruitier, softer, and lighter than Cabernet Sauvignon. Oftentimes, such a description would belittle a wine…or a person for that matter. Such is not the case with Pinot Noir. It is also one of the three or so grapes used in the making of Champagne. Again, Champagne refers to the place in France where sparkling wines are indeed called Champagne. Nowhere else in the world can sparkling wine be called Champagne rightfully. Of course, the message has been slow to spread and a great many of us still use this misnomer when referring to say a Korbel California sparkler.

Pinot Noir prefers a cooler climate than other grapes and such does better in places like Oregon, parts of California, New Zealand and, of course, it's hometown region of Burgundy. When well made a Pinot Noir can be described as graceful elegance dancing in a glass. A cheap Pinot on the other hand is more like falling face forward into a puddle of mud and bland cherries with a significant lack of mud.

CABERNET SAUVIGNON (Please, call me Cab)

Perhaps the wine grape with the most character and biggest range of potential. It is called the king of the reds by some. Others call Pinot Noir the king of the red grapes. Such is the battle between Bordeaux and Burgundy. I will say that Cabernet is the grape with the most attitude. A good bold "cab" is not just in your face, but in your mouth also as you pucker to the tune of its tannins. It can be soft and pleasant as a young wine or grow up to be so complex and full of flavors, it's enough to make a wine snob cry.

Bordeaux in France gave birth to Cabernet. It must have been a breach birth because Cabernet has always needed to be kept in line through blending with a bit of Merlot, Cabernet Franc or other such grapes. Cabernet is the grape most suited to aging. Time can soften some of those hard edges wonderfully. Personally, I find it difficult to buy a wine today for enjoyment seven years from now, but then, buying two bottles could solve that dilemma.

California has adopted Cabernet Sauvignon as its own. Napa Valley, in Napa County, is as famous for its Cabs as New York City is for its cabs. Of course, there are many other places throughout the United States and the world where excellent Cabernet Sauvignon is grown and made. Whereas, Pinot Noir prefers cooler climes and Merlots have a greater climatic tolerance, Cabernet needs some heat for a full ripening. Microwave ovens don't help in making good wine.

MERLOT (Best supporting actor and more)

Merlot's traditional role, at least in Bordeaux, has been to keep its big brother Cabernet in check. The grape has historically been blended with Cabernet so as to soften the edges. Much like Vice President Dick Cheney who provided much insight and guidance to President George W. Bush while remaining largely in the background, Merlot is clearly capable of making great wine on it's own. Chateau Petrus from Bordeaux is perhaps the finest example since it is almost pure

Merlot and one of the most respected and expensive wines in the world.

Merlot has, mainly since the 1980s, grown into the stand-alone wine of great popularity that it deserves to be. There's a California label called "Marilyn Merlot" which has been described as soft and fleshy. The description can be applied to Merlot in general. The skins of the grape are thinner than Cabernet skin which either means that Merlot is more easily offended or the wine is not as tannic. If there was ever a candidate for the everyday wine Merlot might be it.

OTHER WHITE GRAPES

SEMILLON (Like Jimmy Page before Led Zeppelin)

A comparison of this fine grape might be to that of a great studio musician that every other grape respects and wants to perform with. Historically, Semillon has been blended with Sauvignon Blanc in Bordeaux. It's report card reads "an easygoing grape that plays well with others." Semillon does have the characteristic of being susceptible to botrytis, a fungus condition that can attack white wine grapes in certain conditions. Botrytis dries out some of the grapes, leaving a sweet concentration of flavor that, wouldn't you know it, make for some of the finest dessert wines in the world. The French Sauternes are a prime example.

GEWURZTRAMINER (Voted least likely to be ordered in a restaurant)

To order a wine one must be able to pronounce it. I guess you could just point to it on the wine list. Just remember that in German the "w" is pronounced like a "v." Then just add the tram and the inner. Gewurz means spicy. No, it's not a jalapeno wine but the grape does have a bit of pizzazz and pairs well with pizzas. This grape makes for a rich dry wine. There are some however, on the sweet side. The popular offering from Fetzer in California has a bit of a soda pop feel.

Gewurztraminer is known as a French grape with a German name. The Alsace region in France from where it originates is right next to Germany and has in the past been Germany. It's just like the former Governor of California, Arnold Schwarzenegger, who hails from Austria sounding German. That's hail not heil.

Although it's classified as a white grape, the actual skin color is pinkish. The aroma is flowery, "perfumish," and spicy. It is said that either you love it or hate it.

VIOGNIER (The grape that wishes it was as easy to pronounce as Gewurztraminer)

It is not pronounced like vinegar. Viognier is also a wine not frequently ordered in restaurants nor is it frequently carried by most restaurants. A wine of cult status, mainly a California cult status, Viognier has a subtler aroma than Gewurztraminer with the essence of apricot, pear, and maybe a bit of honey. How does that old slogan go again? "You've tried the rest, now try Viognier, "or something like that.

CHENIN BLANC (This grape is noble; no bull)

Chenin Blanc is most common in the cool Loire Valley of France. It's not as popular as many of the other grapes because of a bit of an identity crisis. It can be Sahara dry, made into a dessert wine or into a sparkling wine. As with any other varietal any of these styles can be great or puke. The same wine can be great one year and puke the next. You could even take it a step further from great to puke and back to great with only time as a factor.

PINOT GRIS (GRIGIO that is)

Pinot Grigio is to Pinot Gris as Giuseppe Verde is to Joe Green. Or would that be Joe Greenio? The name comes from the grayish color of the grape. Since we don't want a category other than red or white wine grapes this Pinot falls in with the whites. The Grigio version of this grape is very popular these days. It makes for a light and crisp wine that's easy to drink.

With some exceptions, most wines are easy to drink… after the first two glasses. Gris is the word.

OTHER RED GRAPES

ZINFANDEL (We must pay for our Zins)

A good inexpensive Zinfandel is not easy to find, but the search can be fun. Sometimes it is made into a lighter red wine with a raspberry and peppery taste. Zinfandel can also be as bold and full of character as John Wayne's fist. That is, of course, if his fist was first used to crush some blackberries against an oak tree.

You won't find Zins in France. It's a California grape thought to originate in Italy or Croatia. It also used to be the most widely planted grape in California until Cabernet Sauvignon took over that role. These days, the Zin zone of the wine shoppe is also the wit zone. Names like "7 Deadly Zins," "Cardinal Zin," "Zynthesis," and "Zig Zag Zin," can be found alongside more traditionally labeled Zinfandels such as Seghesio Zinfandel or Clos Du Bois Zinfandel. Oftentimes you'll see the reference "old vine" on Zinfandel labels. The intent here is to imply that since older vines yield fewer grapes and the grapes themselves are more concentrated with Zin flavor you'll have a better wine. Such is usually the case, if you are drinking from a respectable label. Teenage boys trampling grape vines are called "Zin Vandals."

White Zinfandel is made from the Zinfandel grape with much less skin contact. It's like flag football versus real football. Less skin contact accounts for the pink color. It's generally downplayed as not really a wine, but it is and also quite good at times.

SYRAH (Down Under it's Shiraz)

Not to be confused with Petite Syrah which is an altogether different grape. Syrah is the boss grape in Australia. It is also the grape chiefly grown in the Rhône Valley of France. In Australia it is often blended with a bit of Cabernet Sauvignon. The grape itself is very dark and makes for an intense full dark cherry and spicy wine. Syrah is known for its great aging ability in the manner of Methuselah. "Que Syrah Syrah."

GAMAY (You can't have Beaujolais without Gamay)

The lighthearted, fresh, young wine known as Beaujolais comes from the Gamay grape. Gamay in turn comes from Beaujolais the place. It's grown in a few other places as well, but no one cares much about that. The lightest of the red wines comes from this grape. White Zinfandel doesn't count as red wine and to some it doesn't count as a wine at all. With Beaujolais you get no oak, no tannins, and recently I noticed you don't even get glass bottles. Some producers of Beaujolais Nouveau have recently taken to using plastic wine bottles for their product. Call me an old fuddy-duddy, but I prefer wine out of the box. The

Nouveau version is traditionally released in the third week of November. At first it was thought that this release had something to do with the Thanksgiving holiday; I mean you wouldn't want the wine to get old now would you? Of course, it has nothing to do with the American holiday, as it is a French wine. The flavor of this wine is often described as strawberry like.

MALBEC (Don't cry for me)

Although originally from Bordeaux, Malbec has for the most part immigrated to Argentina and is responsible for that country's best wines. If it moved to Argentina some may think that it came from Germany, but that is not the case. Outside of Argentina Malbec is used for blending. The grape is strong and deep in color without a lot of acid.

SANGIOVESE (To say it is very easy)

Italy's most important grape, and responsible for the making of Chianti. Where would Sir Anthony Hopkins be without the Sangiovese grape? Don't you remember that scene in "The Silence of the Lambs" where he describes a human meal that included Fava beans and a nice Chianti? Oh yes, and a human. Sangiovese is also blended with Cabernet Sauvignon. This combination makes for what are called the Super Tuscan wines of where was that? Give me just a minute. Oh yes, Tuscany.

OTHER REDS AND OTHER WHITES

As said earlier there are thousands of other wine grape varietals in the world. We focused on just the same old grapes that most other wine books do. There are so many more that one could write a book about them. It would be a wine bible or world encyclopedia of sorts.

CHAPTER FOUR

WORDS OF WINE

Enology is the study of wine. Geology is the study of rocks. Genealogy is not the study of genies that drink wine. Golly gee is an expression used when one sees the price of so many wines or when considering how on earth some things could possibly get published.

There are as many words and terms related to wine and the description of wine as there are grapes in a vineyard. Some of the following definitions are genuine, whereas others ain't. In other words, they ain't words like some believe ain't ain't a word. What follows is literally a little alliteration liberally littered with a smattering of education.

This glossary is not meant to be all inclusive. It is not even close. After all, they don't fill your glass to the rim at the restaurant do they?.

AFTERTASTE: Flavor remaining in your mouth after wine is swallowed.

AFTERMATH: Too much wine swallowing the night before.

AGING: The maturation process of a wine in either a barrel or bottle.

ANTI AGING: Drinking wine to forget that we are aging.

ALSACE: French appellation or wine region in France known for excellent white wines.

ALLSAUCED: What you're likely to be after downing a bottle of wine in 15 minutes.

APPELLATION: A geographical region known for growing wine grapes.

APPALACHIA: A culturally geographic region not known for growing wine grapes. Although, plenty of good wine is made here.

AROMA: The scent of a wine before it matures into a bouquet, or a kind of tomato.

AVA: American Viticultural Area. This abbreviation denotes standard geographic appellation classifications in the United States. Example: AVA Napa Valley or AVA Gardner. Well, maybe not the Gardner one.

BACCHUS: The Roman god of wine and a grape widely planted in Germany.

BACCHUS ACHEOUS: Ailment from picking grapes all day long.

BALANCE: The harmonious coming together of all of a wine's elements such as acidity, alcohol, sweetness, dryness, oak, tannins and such. It is also, that which is lost after excessive harmonious coming together of a wine's elements.

BARBERA: Italian grape used alone or blended with other grapes in California. This could also refer to one half of the creative duo that brought us Yogi Bear, Huckleberry Hound and many other famous characters.

BARBARIC: The behavior of customers when a "free" wine tasting is announced.

BARREL: Wooden vessel (made from oak) used for fermentation and/or aging of wine. (A barrel of wine is more fun and tastes better than a barrel of monkeys).

BEAUJOLAIS: The wine region in the southern part of Burgundy known for its non-oaky, non-tannin, non-"in your face" red wine from the Gamay grape. Not to be confused with Beau Joe Lazy from the southern part of Oklahoma who IS in your face, tanned, and oaky.

BEAUJOLAIS NOUVEAU: This is not "new and improved" Beaujolais with Techron added for better performance, but rather a young red wine from the region released on the third Thursday each November after the harvest.

BEAULIEU: Well respected Napa Valley Winery. (Sometimes referred to as BV) Please don't confuse this with BVD. The former has a much better bouquet.

BERINGER VINEYARDS: Well respected Napa winery and historic building. (It is never referred to as BV).

BERNKASTEL: A German village with some of the best and steepest vineyards. It is known for producing quality Riesling.

BURN CASTLE: What the villagers wanted to do in the "Frankenstein" movies.

BLANC: French word meaning white.

BLANCO: Spanish word meaning white.

BLANK: Inability to come up with a joke for blanc and blanco.

BLANC DE BLANCS: Sparkling wine made from white grapes only. Literally, it means white from white, but there doesn't appear to be a segregationist purpose behind it.

BLANC DE NOIRS: Sparkling wine made from mostly red grapes. Note: A sparkling wine made with just any old grapes is called "Fillin de blanc."

BLUSH: A term for rose' wines coined in California. Some good pink wines like White Zinfandel used to get a bum rap by being associated with the likes of cheap pink jug wines. Contrary to some belief blush has nothing to do with being a lush.

BODY: Involving wine, it refers to the fullness when tasted. The body increases with alcohol content. It was previously thought that the body increased with chocolate cake content.

BORDEAUX: Wine-growing region in western France considered the "downtown" of fine wine. This is the Mercedes Benz of wine regions. Some may think that calling it the "Peugeot" of wine regions would be more appropriate, but we wouldn't want to offend anyone. Too late.

BOTRYTIS CINERIA: Scientific name for Noble Rot which is the layperson's term for a fungus that attacks some white wine grapes making for a better wine. It sounds a little like a waiter saying, "the fly is supposed to be in the soup."

BOUQUET: A block of charcoal used in grilling food. Oh wait, that's briquet. Bouquet is the smell a wine has after it's been in the bottle for a time. Some of us have an uncle that develops a bouquet after being ON the bottle for a time, but that's different.

BOX WINES: Finally, there's a wine selection that you can just throw in the back of the truck. In actuality and fairness, some of these are quite good. Just be sure to keep them to a minimum and hopefully, out of sight from the guests.

BRIX: This is not a circumcision, but rather a system of measuring the sugar content of wine grapes at harvest using degrees. See residual sugar and residual penis.

BRUT: The French term for sparkling wine that's drier than Extra Dry. There is also an "Extra Brut" category. The only thing drier would be an empty bottle. Beyond extra brut there is only O J Simpson.

BULL'S BLOOD: Short for the most famous Hungarian wine "Bulls Blood of Eger." Surprisingly it's made from the kekfrankos grape and contains neither blood nor bull…unlike this book.

BURGUNDY: Formerly synonymous with cheap California red jug wine. Before formerly, this grand wine region in eastern central France was and is renowned for its reds made from Pinot Noir and whites made from Chardonnay. The French pronunciation (Bourgogne) is great to throw around at family gatherings if you don't mind getting slapped with mashed potatoes.

CABERNET FRANC: This is not a term like Budweiser Joe or Chardonnay Jane, but rather one of the five red grape varietals in Bordeaux wines used chiefly in blending with Cabernet Sauvignon or Merlot.

CABERNET SAUVIGNON: King of the red grapes it is called. From Bordeaux to California to Australia, Argentina, Chile and elsewhere, this grape is responsible for some of the world's finest wines. Is there a message in that a king is at his best only after being crushed and left to rot? Hmmm.

CARBON DIOXIDE: A gaseous by-product of the fermentation process. This gas is what is trapped in the bottles of sparkling wines resulting in the bubbles. We'll pass on a gas joke here.

CARBONIC MACERATION: A process of fermenting grapes while still whole. By not crushing the grapes the wine is ready sooner and is far lower in tannins making for easier drinking. Sounds like impatience. Why not just eat some grapes while sipping brandy?

CARIGNAN: Not a type of sweater, but rather a grape from Spain where it has a, what do you know, a Spanish name (Carinena or Mazuelo).

CARNEROS: An AVA in California including parts of Napa and Sonoma Counties. The conditions here are perfect for growing Pinot Noir and Chardonnay. Not to be confused with Carnitas for which the conditions are almost always perfect with cilantro, onions, corn tortillas, salsa, and beer.

CARMANARE: A grape from the Medoc in Bordeaux that emigrated to Chile where it tried passing for Merlot until it was found out. Many immigrants can relate to this.

CASK: A barrel that's larger than a barrel. Edgar Allan Poe had some fine sherry in his. If a deceased person was placed in one of these, it would be called a "casket".

CAVA: Spanish sparkling wine made using the Champagne method.

CELLAR: Not a vendor of wine, but rather a place where wine is stored. One's bladder is not considered a temporary wine cellar.

CHABLIS: The winemaking region in northern Burgundy where excellent Chardonnay is produced.

CHALBIS: A typographically incorrect printing of Chablis.

CHAMPAGNE: The AC (Appellation d'Origine Controlee) in northern France famous for sparkling wine. Only the sparkling wine made here can be called Champagne. Of course, Americans don't usually give a hill of beans, or grapes for that matter, what the French want so we call most if not all sparkling wine champagne.

CHAPTALIZATION: The process of adding sugar to crushed grapes. This is done either before or during fermentation for the purpose of raising the alcohol content. Next thing you know they'll be adding cream along with the sugar to make breakfast wine.

CHARBONO: Nothing to do with Cher when she was married to Sonny. It is a red wine grape used in wine production, but not commonly.

CHARDONNAY: A great grape, a great wine and who knows? It could possibly be the next popular name for newborn girls. The boys already have Bud as a name so it's only fair.

CHATEAU: A French word meaning castle. It also refers to wine estates such as Chateau St. Jean in Kenwood, California.

CHATEAU LAFITE-ROTHSCHILD: Famous red wine from Pauillac in Bordeaux. It sounds very fancy doesn't it? On the rare occasion that this wine is not great, the producers are said to be suffering from 'the agony of Lafite."

CHATEAU LATOUR: Another classic French wine also from Pauillac in Bordeaux. Not to be confused with that really awful wine called Chateau LeTurd.

CHATEAU PETRUS: Commonly known as one of the most expensive wines in the world. It is made from the Merlot grape in Pomerol, Bordeaux. Also, since most of the real famous and expensive red wines tend to be Cabernet Sauvignon, Chateau Petrus carries the added distinction of going "nanananana" to Cabernets.

CHATEAUNEUF-DU-PAPE: The coolest sounding French wine term. It's not only fun to say, but happens to be an excellent wine growing region in the Rhone Valley of France. The term means new castle of the Pope.

CHENIN BLANC: Often confused with Cheney Blanc which some far left media pundits say the former Vice President used to secretly influence American foreign policy, but this is an entirely different type of white wine. It is also better appreciated.

CHIANTI: You're tempted to drop the "nti" from this wine just so that you can say Ch Ch Ch Chia, but it doesn't work. The "ch" is pronounced like a "k". Perhaps a jingle could be produced and sold to the

Korean car manufacturer. Ki Ki Ki Kia! We di di di gress. This important red wine from Tuscany in Italy is known as a great food wine. It is made from the Sangiovese grape.

CHILE: A very hot pepper such as Jalapeno or Habanero known to make people say "Ay Caramba." It is also a term to signify that it is not warm or a stew consisting of meat, beans, tomatoes, spices and more. (Hold the beans in Texas). By chance it also refers to a long skinny coastal country in South America with a very good and bettering reputation for producing fine wines.

CLARET: An English word referring to the wines of Bordeaux. Not normal English, but rather English from England.

CLOS: In French it means a vineyard that is walled or enclosed by walls. In America it means that some child has difficulty spelling Santa's full name.

CLOS DU BOIS: The very popular winery out of Sonoma County or the walling in of Blanche by the actions of one Stanley Kowalski.

CLOUDY BAY: A very general term meaning that the bay such as San Francisco Bay or Emerald Bay has clouds about it. By the way, it also refers to the first winery from New Zealand to receive recognition from other countries for its Sauvignon Blanc.

COLLIO DOC: Not to be confused with Collie DOG. Collio is a region in Italy where some of that country's best wines come from.

CONCENTRATE: Either the "just add water" to restore a juice to its original state or trying to stay on your side of the road in traffic.

CORK: What some would suggest wiseacres put in.

CORKAGE: The price YOU have to pay to have YOUR wine opened and served at a restaurant. The next thing you know there will be a rental fee for the use of a fork. Refuse to pay a forking rental fee. By the way, the corkage process has been known to cause the line at the drive-thru to back up.

COTE: If it were cold outside you wouldn't put this on. This is the French term for either a hillside or slope. Many ACs (appellations; not air conditioning) are named after cotes such as Cote De Nuits, Cote D Or, and Cote Rotie. Not part of this group is Coat De Jacquet.

CRU: This French term means either a vineyard, or a wine estate, or even a chateau. It is also key to the classification of French wines. You'll hear some terms such as Premier Cru, Grand Cru, Cru Bourgeois, and Cru of the SS Minnow.

CRUSH: This has nothing to do with neither orange nor affectionate leanings, nor even the stock market in 1929. Crush is what happens to a grape before it can become wine. Of course, there's more involved than just that. If you were to step on a grape and leave it there on your boot, it may not become wine. Besides, it's very difficult to get a boot in a bottle.

CUVEE: This either has to do with blending grapes such as in Champagne or the French equivalent of "Oy vey."

DECANT: The process of pouring the poor wine into a pourer for the purpose of pouring it.

DEMI-SEC: A medium dry wine. Yes, it's a French term such as demitasse, and Demi Moore.

DESSERT WINE: Please do not put whipped cream in your wine. These wines are already sweet and usually served with guess which course of the meal?

DESSERT TORTOISE: One who pours sweet wine very slowly in the Sahara.

DOLCE: How sweet to finally see a term that isn't French.

DOMAINE: The French term meaning estate. In real estate it means that the eminent government could take your chateau and the land on which it sits leaving you with sour grapes.

DRY: Humor dispensed in a subtle, often sarcastic way. It is sometimes witty and sometimes knit witty. It could also refer to a wine that isn't dolce.

DULCE: Spanish word for dolce; not dry.

EARTHY: A person who tastes wine while wearing Birkenstock sandals. It is also a term to favorably describe the taste of some wine but nonetheless dirty. Many children are familiar with this taste.

EISWEIN: German super scientist famous for his theory of relativity. Oh wait, that's Einstein. Eiswein refers to a very sweet wine made from grapes left on the vine to freeze. Being left out in the cold is sometimes a good thing. Be careful using this term in the South because due to the accents it comes out "ass wine" and you really don't want to taste that.

ESTATE BOTTLED: When you see this term on a label it means that the wine was bottled in the same location where the grapes were grown. Some of the grapes have been heard to say, "You never take me anywhere!"

ETHANOL: The alcohol whose percentage appears on the wine label. This is not to be confused with methanol whose aroma is commonly experienced in cow pastures.

EXTRA DRY: When absolutely no one laughs because they didn't get it. It could also mean a wine that is not as dry as Brut and certainly not as dry as Extra Brut. To be brutally honest extra dry isn't sweet. Of course, neither is being brutally honest.

FERMENTATION: The scientific process by which yeast converts the sugar in grapes into ethanol. For such a wonderful process there should be an equally flattering term such as "hoochification" or "boozilation."

FATTORIA: Italian word meaning domain. Many confuse this with skinnyoria, tortilleria, and diarrhea; none of which have anything to do with wine. The owner of the fattoria is considered "domain man."

FIDDLETOWN: The pompous sounding AVA (wine region) in Amador County California. This area is known for producing excellent Zinfandel.

FINING: What the judge can do to you along with incarceration and license suspension if you get caught drinking and driving so don't drink and drive. It also refers to the process of clarifying wine by adding things such as egg whites (seriously).

FIRST GROWTH: You might think that this refers to the oldest grape in the bunch, but it actually refers to the top category of Bordeaux wines. See also Premier Cru.

FLUTE: The recommended glass for sipping sparkling wines. Its design is not based on the breast of Marie Antoinette as supposedly are those shallow Champagne glasses. Many jokes and inferences have been made about the body part responsible for the flute's design so we won't put ours in. It is true, however, that the bubbles last longer in the flute making for a more sparkling sparkling wine experience.

FORTIFIED WINES: This has nothing to do with bodily functions after bean consumption nor does it refer to wines stored at The Alamo in San Antonio, Texas. Wines that have been given an alcohol boost such as Port, Sherry, Madeira and such are fortified wines.

FREE-RUN: The juice from a grape that runs or drains even though the grape has not been crushed or pressed. It sounds a bit like a leak doesn't it?

FREE RANGE: A chicken that runs before being pressed.

FRANCE: The country responsible for many of the terms appearing in this glossary. They know a thing or two about wine as well.

FRENCH PARADOX: What some people use to convince themselves that they can eat all of the Brie, whipped cream, bacon, cheeseburgers, fries and still be healthy as long as they wash it all down with a barrel of wine. It actually refers to research finding that even though the French diet is generally higher in fat than that of other cultures they have a lower incidence of heart disease. This is attributed to their daily consumption of red wine. Keep in mind the size of French portions however. They don't have triple bacon guacamole cheeseburgers served up with chocolate shakes.

FRUITY: When a wine tastes like it originated from fruit it is considered fruity. When it tastes like it originated from feet then it is considered funky.

FUMÉ BLANC: Wine made from Sauvignon Blanc but with a marketing department behind it. The legendary California winemaker Robert Mondavi coined this term to sell more Sauvignon Blanc.

GALLO: Ernest and Julio Gallo are said to be responsible for about one fourth of the United States wine sales. They must be tired and have a big truck. Since the end of Prohibition when they began making wine, sometimes of questionable quality, this company has grown to be the largest winemaker in the world. Gallo owns among many others, Barefoot Cellars, Andre, Turning Leaf, Carlo Rossi, Boone's Farm, and of course, the highly respected Gallo of Sonoma.

GAMAY: The grape without which there would be no Beaujolais. Of course, there would still be thousands of other wine to choose from so it's not such a big deal unless you like Beaujolais or "New and Improved Beaujolais." I mean Beaujolais Nouveau.

GERMANY: Famed European country not known for French wine terms. Their Rieslings, cars, sausages, and scientists are known to be among the world's best.

GEWURZTRAMINER: This sounds like it would be a gastrointestinal condition caused by bacteria found on the feet of Dachshunds, but it isn't. This white wine can be dry or sweet, but with a characteristic of spice in the flavor. Gewurz is actually German for spice. A good example of this wine is worth seeking out. The Alsace in France is known to make great ones. Not Dachshunds, but Gewurztraminers.

GRAN RESERVA: The term in Spain for the best and rarest of wines from the best vineyards. They are aged more than the Spanish Crianzas and Reservas.

GRAND CRU: This French term for great growth makes it sound like it would refer to the best wines, but it's not that simple. The whole French classification system can be rather confusing. In addition to Grand Cru there is Premier Cru, Premier Grand Cru, Bourgeois Cru, Deuxieme Cru, Cinquieme Cru and more. Perhaps they could benefit from a Cru cut.

GRAND OPENING: American term for when a third rate celebrity or local government official cuts a ribbon using oversized scissors at the opening of a new retail establishment. It has nothing to do with wine unless the retailer is Costco Wholesale, BevMo, Total Wine or the like.

GRAPE: A smooth skinned berry ranging in color from light greenish to deep dark purple without whom this book would be nothing but blanc pages. Wine critics would whine, wine stewards would stew, and winos wouldn't know.

GRAPIST: Someone who rips out a grape vineyard and plants condominiums.

GRENACHE: The classic American sitcom "Green Acres" translated loosely, very loosely, into French. It is also a red wine grape used in France, Spain, Australia, and the United States with small plantings in Pixley and Hooterville.

HAUT-MEDOC: The AOC or "Appellation d'Origen Controlee" in Bordeaux which is home to some of the most famous wine communes and appellations.

HERMITAGE: Yet another appellation in France. This one is in the northern Rhone area and also is famous for producing great red wines. Could it possibly be just one guy running things and he lives alone?

HOT: Hopefully, sales of this book. In wine terms, however, it refers to wines tasting out of balance due to excessive alcohol. The sensation, wouldn't you know, is one of burning.

HUNGARY: Often overlooked home to more than goulash. Hungarian whiplash occurs when stopping suddenly in front of a winery producing fine Tokay.

ICEWINE: See Eiswein. It does not suggest putting ice cubes in wine. This could be interpreted as asking for a slap.

IRRIGATION: This is not as much a wine term as it is an agricultural term. It refers to the process of getting water to where it needs to be for plant growth and fruit production. Surprisingly, this is not permitted in the classic French regions of Burgundy and Bordeaux.

IRRITATION: What the grapes of Burgundy and Bordeaux must feel when learning that all of the other grapes in the world get irrigated.

ITALY: This country and not France is the leading producer of wine in the world. Previously known for spaghetti wines, spaghetti westerns, and spaghetti spaghetti, vast improvements have elevated Italy to world-class quality. Carlo Rossi would be proud.

JADOT, LOUIS: A leading wine producer out of Burgundy. They offer a wide range of wines, red and white, with reliable quality across a vast price range. You can pick up their Beaujolais at your local grocer for $12 or the Clos Vougoet for just under $200, although not likely at your local grocer. Note: if you were to combine both bottles and then split the result they would not be worth $106 each.

JAMMY: What one wears when going to bed. It also refers to the thick concentrated flavor of some wines. Many Zinfandels are commonly described this way.

JUG WINE: The most refined, highly regarded, rare and sought after wine in the world…not.

KABINETT: A ranking of German wines on one of their scales based on ripeness. These wines are usually stored in the kitchen.

KOSHER WINE: Not as you might think (any wine with a cup of sugar stirred in), but rather one produced under a Rabbi's supervision.

KRUG: Legendary and ridiculously expensive Champagne. Each grape used in this prestigious beverage undergoes an extensive background check. You can easily spend $200, $400 and then some for this fizzy grape juice. It's probably pretty good though.

KRUG, CHARLES: Known as the first winery in Napa Valley. It was established in 1861 by none other than Charles Krug. Since the 1950s the winery has been run by the Peter Mondavi family. Incredibly, unlike the French Krug, the Napa Krugs manage to produce good wine at less than $25 a bottle.

LAMBRUSCO: The first wine many of us ever tried. It could have been strawberry soda; make that artificial strawberry soda. This Italian grape is also made into a dry red wine.

LANGUEDOC-ROUSSILLON: Next to Chateauneuf Du Pape, this is the second coolest sounding wine area of France.

LATE HARVEST: When you have to work overtime to finish picking the grapes because some coworkers called in sick. On the bright side, the grapes are sweeter due to the extra hang time.

LEES: Either my favorite brand of blue jeans or the sediment found at the bottom of the wine barrel after fermentation. This sediment is a good thing in wine as it adds complexity. Sediment also adds complexity if found in your jeans, though not in a good way.

LEGS: The tracks of wine on the side of the glass after a sip. Whoever thought this term up was probably preoccupied with other thoughts at the time.

LIEBFRAUMILCH: Very popular sweetish German wine. I guess that's better than a germish Sweden wine. It is largely exported because the Germans are smart enough to keep the good wine there at home. The literal translation is "dear mother's milk."

LOIRE: Though not as famous as Bordeaux and Burgundy, this large wine-growing region is also known for excellent wines red, white, pink and bubbly. These include Sancerre (sincerely), Vouvray (hooray), Chinon (possibly a Chinese blend), and Pouilly-Fumé (does not mean chicken fumes).

MACERATION: The "let sleeping dogs lie" of red winemaking so to speak. Grape skins, pulp, juice and such are left alone in fermentation to give red wines color and tannins. It follows that the longer the sleeping dogs lay the darker the wine.

MADEIRA: A fortified wine of Portugal. In the production process the wine is heated thereby giving it a burnt taste. They may just be saying that it's supposed to taste that way like my mother said about her rice.

MAIPO VALLEY: One of Chile's most important wine growing regions. Some may confuse it with the state of Maine, famous for its "maipo" syrup.

MALBEC: After the war many Europeans moved to South America. This grape moved from Bordeaux to Argentina where it has become that country's most important red wine. In France it was just a bit player among the four other grapes used there.

MALOLACTIC FERMENTATION: The secondary fermentation that most wines go through in the barrel whereby the harsh malic acid get converted into lactic acid. Call it puberty for wine. At this stage some wines think that they know everything, but don't.

MARGAUX: French AC (appellation controlee) in the famous Haut-Medoc area of the Bordeaux region. Don't foregeaux Margaux Bordeaux when to France you geaux.

MARLBOROUGH: The wine region of New Zealand's South Island known for producing that country's best Sauvignon Blanc. Every winemaker there calls himself the Marlborough Man.

MARSALA: A couple of famous musicians, Wynton and Branford, known for producing great jazz. Oh, wait a minute. That would be Marsalis'. Marsala must be some not so famous anymore fortified Italian wine used in some cooking.

MASSON, PAUL: A real person from Burgundy, France that moved to California in the 1870s or so and made wine. His wine and sparkling wines were made in the Santa Clara Valley area of California now known more for Silicon than grapes. Masson's commercial slogan in the 1970s as delivered by Orson Welles is one of the most remembered in history. "We will sell no wine before its time." That time, by the way, was as soon as the stores opened in the morning.

MASTER OF WINE: The Institute of Masters of Wine based in London confers upon those qualified this designation of MW. It is said that this level of achievement involving rigorous education, rigorous writing and even more rigorous tasting is more difficult than becoming a sommelier or a master sommelier. Others of us settle for a VW.

MATURATION: Accepting that many of us may never achieve the Master of Wine qualification nor be able to sip wine such as Château Petrus with regularity. Just appreciating regularity is a sign of maturation.

MENDOCINO COUNTY: California's stepsister wine county to Napa and Sonoma. Mendocino produces various fine wines, both red and white depending on the microclimate. It is also home to some of California's most beautiful coastline, at least until the state falls into the ocean.

MENDOZA: Not Argentinean for Mendocino, but rather the heart of Argentinean wine production. This region produces about three fourths of the country's wine. The country is the fifth largest producer of wine in the world. That's a lotta Malbec plus.

MERLOT: Marilyn's last name. Not really, although there is a wine labeled "Marilyn Merlot." This great grape often plays second fiddle to Cabernet Sauvignon in popularity, but has gained much respect over the years due to its softer touch.

MICROCLIMATE: When it rains just a little bit.

MOET & CHANDON: The world's largest producer of Champagne and home to the likes of Dom Perignon. The champagne, that is, not the Benedictine Monk for which it is named after. He moved out hundreds of years ago. Domaine Chandon out of Napa Valley is owned by Moet & Chandon. The name makes it sound like it comes from France as would for example, Domaine Brooklyn.

MONDAVI, ROBERT: One of, if not the biggest name in California wine during the 20th century. Before passing in May 2008 he passed along to the world technical innovations, wine marketing innovations and good wine. He was to wine as Tommy Lasorda is to baseball.

MONTRACHET: This does not refer to a mountain of ratchets. For starters the first t is silent. For enders the second t is silent and the "e" is pronounced like an "a." This Burgundy appellation produces what many believe to be the best white wine (in Burgundy this means Chardonnay) in the world.

MOSCATO: This grape is called Muscat in English and Moscatel in Spanish. Don't confuse it with muskrat, which isn't as sweet.

MOSEL-SAAR-RUWER: Three rivers much like in Pittsburg, Pennsylvania, although these are in Germany. Some of the best Rieslings in the world come from here. The best of these best originate along the Mosel River.

MOUNT VEEDER: If the French can have Montrachet and those other famous ACs, then California can have Mount Veeder in Napa County. If it says Mount Veeder on the label, you can bet that it's a good wine and not $4.99 a bottle.

MOURVEDRE: This red wine grape pops up every now and then, but not as much as others. Less is Mourvedre.

MULLER-THURGAU: The name implies anything from a fine German furniture maker, to a legal firm in Philadelphia, to an inoperable disorder of the Muller gland. It is actually a German white grape.

MUST: When you look at the sole of your shoe after having stepped on some grapes you see must. It includes the juice, pulp, seeds, and stem of the grapes once crushed. This is a must know.

NAPA VALLEY: America's Bordeaux or the most famous AVA in the western hemisphere. Did you know that they grow auto parts here as well?

NEBBIOLO: Although it's one of the world's great red wine grapes responsible for Barolo, Barbaresco and other fine Italian wines, it is not as well known outside of that country. The reason is nebulous.

NEW ZEALAND: Island country, actually, a multi-island country with a new zeal for fine wine. Known mostly for its Sauvignon Blanc, this country produces wine from the other major varietals as well.

NOBLE GRAPES: The eight or nine or some other smallish number of wine grapes considered to be the classic wine grapes. The number is expanding as more and more grapes get voted into this hall of fame.

NOBLE ROT: No, not this book. It isn't noble enough. The term refers to Botrytis Cineria defined earlier. It's also what happened to Lancelot's sword after he kept leaving it out in the rain.

NOBLE BOOK: Karen MacNeil's *The Wine Bible* from Workman Publishing Company, Inc. This well written wine resource will educate one properly in all things wine. It's a lotta book. There is no affiliation between Workman Publishing and Playing With Wine. Perhaps soon.

NO BULL: What the spinster cow in the field was heard to say, or rather, moo.

NOSE: Instead of saying smell, scent, odor, or aroma when sniffing a wine some prefer to use the word nose. Example: "This wine is a bit big on the nose." It means that many scents are emanating from the glass. Or it could just mean that he's using too small glass for the size of his nose.

NOUVEAU: The opposite of oldveau. Chic French wine term for new. Remember when chic used to be a nouveau French term?

OAK: It's a tree; duh.

OAKY: However tempting it may be to say, oaky wines do not come from Oklahoma. Wines aged in oak barrels take on flavors of the oak and are thus called oaky. When the oak and wine balance really well as in some higher priced Chardonnays it is said to be oaky doky.

OFF DRY: Wine that is not really sweet and not really dry. It's like when you try to show your wife how helpful you are and attempt to do some laundry. You can't wait for the dryer to finish so the clothes aren't totally dry and you ruin some of her garments in the process so it's not really sweet.

OLD VINES: This term is most commonly seen on Zinfandel labels. Supposedly the older the vines the more concentrated the flavors since fewer grapes are produced. How old is old we couldn't say, but if it has to do with wine the vines must be adults.

OLOROSO: Basically, there are two types of sherry, the fortified wine from Spain. Fino is one and oloroso is the other. Just by the name, fino sounds fine and oloroso sounds like someone got carried away with the vowels as in Alabama, Mississippi, and heebie-jeebies.

OPUS ONE: Expensive and much hyped collaborative wine effort made by Baron Philippe de Rothschild and Robert Mondavi. It's a good blend of the Bordeaux grapes. Perhaps the sequel will be better and less expensive.

OVER CROPPING: A symptom displayed when one suffers from an upset stomach also referred to a diarrhea. Or would that be overcrapping? If so, why would you want to display it? Actually, it refers to when vines aren't thinned resulting in watered down grapes so to speak.

OXIDATION: A wine that has hyperventilated is said to be suffering from oxidation. As with most things moderation is the key, be it wine or breathing.

PALATE: The roof of a person's mouth as well as the sense of taste and reaction to that being tasted. The person you share wine with is your "copalate" which was first heard on an episode of M*A*S*H.

PALOMINO: This is not a wine made from horses but rather the name of a white wine grape from Spain used in the making of sherry. They say that the best of these Sherries is called Palomino Fino. Wouldn't Fino Palomino Vino have a better ring?

PARDUCCI: Well respected California winemaker or an Italian poker term meaning a pair of twos.

PAUILLAC: French AC that would not even be included in this glossary due to pronunciation issues were it not so famous for producing some of the world's best wines. It lies in the Haut-Medoc region of Bordeaux.

PEDRO XIMENEX: Southern California landscaper that trimmed my palm trees for $20 a tree. Wait, that's spelled with a J. Ximenex is the Spanish grape highly important in the production of Sherry.

PENFOLDS: Huge Australian wine producer established in 1844. It is known for producing that country's most famous Shiraz "Grange." It should not be confused with "Grunge" from Pigpenfolds.

PERIGNON, DOM: Not only is it very famous Champagne, but a real person. Dom was a Benedictine Monk who lived from 1639 to 1715 in Champagne, France of course. He is credited with vastly improving the production of the wine beginning with the vines. It is said that he never drank wine. This is easily understood given that monks usually take a vow of poverty and that this Champagne sells for $200 a bottle.

PETITE SIRAH: This red wine grape is not Syrah's little sister. They may not even be that closely related. For being petite, however, this wine can pack a punch.

PFALZ: It is true that Pfalz is a wine region of Germany. It is false that Pfalz makes the best German wines though some are true to Riesling.

PHYLLOXERA: It doesn't sound good does it? The Wine Guide from Williams-Sonoma calls it a "root eating louse that lives in the soil. It chews away at vine roots until the vine eventually dies from lack of water and nourishment." Many families include a member fitting this description. "Thank you for coming over. Say hello to our phylloxera."

PIEDMONT: Important wine region of Italy where wines such as Barolo and Barbaresco among others are made.

PINOT GRIGIO: The Italian and more common name for the white wine grape Pinot Gris (pronounced "gree" and not "grease"). A wine named after the author might be called Pinot Gregio.

PINOT MEUNIER: Although it sounds as if this would be a fertilizer made from peanuts it is not. This red wine grape is one of the three grapes used in the production of Champagne.

PINOT NOIR: Whereas Bordeaux has Cabernet Sauvignon and Merlot, Burgundy has this grape as its king of the reds. It's a fussy little grape. So much so that it might be better called a princess. All conditions have to be just right for a great Pinot Noir.

PLONK: This English term, not an American term, used to mean bad wine and now it just means basic everyday wine. Of course, if your basic everyday wine happens to be Chateau Petrus then plonk means great expensive wine.

POMACE: A pulpy mass as opposed to a mass from the pulpit. In other words, it is what remains after grapes are crushed and have fermented. Don't confuse this with pumice which refers to smelly mice; maybe not.

POMEROL: French home of the world's most expensive wine, Chateau Petrus. Some pretty fussy Pomeranians live there as well, to be sure.

PORT: Where accommodating women go to meet incoming sailors. It also refers to the sweet fortified wine from Portugal.

POUILLY-FUISSE: A French AC and term almost as fun to say as Chateauneuf Du Pape. The wines are Chardonnay.

POUILLY-FUMÉ: The fumes that emanate from those who overindulge in Pouilly-Fuisse and bad cheese.

PRADIKAT: The German equivalent to the English terms Fraidy-cat or scaredy-cat. It also has to do with wine quality based on sugar levels and such.

PREMIER CRU: The people that roll out the red carpets and keep the fans behind the ropes at major movie openings. It is also one of many quality levels of French appellations.

PRESS: Equipment that separates the grape juice from the grape through the use of pressure and those people that always give politicians a hard time through the use of pressure.

PRIMITIVO: Very early version of a digital video recorder. This term also refers to a red wine grape from Italy that many believe is the same as California Zinfandel.

PROHIBITION: A mere suggestion by the United States government in the 1920s and early 1930s.

PROSECCO: An Italian grape usually made into a sparkling wine, but not by amateurs.

PUNT: What you do when it's fourth down and still ten yards to go. This also refers to the indentation in the bottom of some wine bottles for the collection of sediment, for the illusion of more wine remaining in the bottle than there really is and for some idiot to put his thumb while pouring to appear cool. You know he's going to spill some. What an idiot.

QBA: Qualitatswein betsimmer Anbaugebiete. As if it needed some explanation.

QMP: Qualitatswein mit Pradikat. This refers to one of the farmer's best pigs (quality swine) that somehow put on mittens and scared the cat, but it could also mean something completely different.

RACKING: The setting up of the billiard balls before the break and a process of separating wine from its sediment. It is the equivalent of changing a wine's diaper so to speak.

RAPEL VALLEY: You may think that this is an area of Chile where heinous crimes are committed, but it isn't. They actually produce fine Cabernets, Merlots and other wines in this part of Chile.

RESERVA: What you do to a table so as to guarantee seating at a restaurant. It is also Portuguese and Spanish for wines of above average quality.

RESERVE: If you see this term on a bottle of American wine, buy it fast because there are probably only a few billion other bottles like it. In all fairness, sometimes it really is set aside and of outstanding quality.

RESIDUAL SUGAR: The amount of sugar remaining in a wine after fermentation.

RESIDUAL PENIS: The amount of penis remaining after a circumcision.

RESVERATROL: You know that thing in red wine that allows you eat bacon cheeseburgers, chocolate cakes, banana splits, and pizzas like there's no tomorrow? This is that antioxidant. You should watch it though, because there may be no tomorrow.

RHEINHESSEN: Large German wine producing region in Germany of all places.

RHONE VALLEY: This French wine region is not as famous as Bordeaux or Burgundy, but it is right up there as far as wine quality. It follows the Rhone River and would have been more famous than Bordeaux had it not been at the Rhone place and the Rhone time.

RICH: What you would have to be to try many of these wines.

RIESLING: To look at the word one may think of two combatants trying to pin each other in an athletic competition. That's wrestling. Remember "i before e except after c." In wine it's white before red except just before bed." Some wines of this noble white grape could qualify as desert wines and others are dry. Then there are those in between. All are worth trying.

RIOJA DOC: Not a Spanish doctor specializing in wine injuries, but rather an appellation in northern Spain.

RISERVA: Italian term meaning reserve or reserva. For example, you go into an Italian restaurant and the host asks "Did you riserva table?"

ROOTSTOCK: A wine themed music festival held on some farm in New York back in the late 1960s. It was reported that numerous wines got some bad acid.

ROSÉ: Rhymes with José, but not hose or nose. It's when you start out making a red wine and lose patience. The winemaker removes the skins from the fermenting wine early because he has an appointment. The result is a light pink to light red wine marketed strictly to nurses and secretaries.

ROSSO: The Italian word for red as are rossi and rossa. Why not russo while we're at it? Maybe it's Russian for red.

ROTHSCHILD, BARON PHILIPPE DE: One of the most influential men of wine in the 20th century. He is responsible for building one of the most successful wine brands in the world (Mouton Cadet) and collaborated with Robert Mondavi on the famous Opus One venture. He was born in 1902 and aged until 1988.

ROUGE: French for rosso or rojo or red as well as some sort of makeup. Some have been known to use so much that it's enough to make you blush.

ROGUE: A newer AVA in southern Oregon that must have been named after some idiot clerk misspelled rouge on the application for AVAs. Just a theory.

RUBY CABERNET: A wine grape created by crossing Cabernet Sauvignon not with rubies, but rather with Carignan. It sounds better and is easier to order a glass of Ruby Cab as opposed to Carignan Sauvignon.

RUTHERFORD AVA: An AVA in Napa Valley known for producing world-class wine, particularly Cabernets.

SACHSEN: A wine region in northern Germany known for dry wines from Muller-Thurgau and other grapes. Some have been known to incorrectly link Sachsen to drugs and rock n roll. (In case you're wondering Ian Drury and the Blockheads had a song in the late 70s or early 80s called "Sex and Drugs and Rock n Roll."

SACRAMENTAL WINE: Wine used for religious ceremonies in Judeo Christian faiths.

SACRIFICIAL WINE: When there's just a little bit left in the bottle and you leave it for the other person.

SACRAMENTO WINE: Wine brought over from a Napa or Sonoma County Winery a mere couple of hours away that could have been purchased for much less at a local grocery store.

SANCERRE: This appellation in the Loire Valley region of France is known for fine wine from the Sauvignon Blanc grape. It is said that wines from this region should be drunk young, but it is probably better to wait until you're of legal drinking age. Sancerrely yours.

SANGIOVESE: This is one of the most widely planted grapes in Italy and is often blended with Cabernet Sauvignon. The Super Tuscans are made with this grape. The pooper Tuscans are made with inferior grapes.

SASSICAIA: This Super Tuscan wine belongs in any glossary just based on appearance. Nevertheless, we are not always successful in saying something sassy. It is not as easy as Sangiovese so see ya'.

SAUTERNES: This appellation in Bordeaux produces a dessert wine which is one of the world's most famous (Chateau d'Yquem).

SAUVIGNON BLANC: One of the great white grapes. This versatile grape makes for different styles of wine depending on whether it's made in the Loire Valley France, California, or New Zealand which has been very successful with it. Fumé Blanc is Sauvignon Blanc with a Hollywood name coined by the late Robert Mondavi.

SEC: This is French for "trocken" which is German for "seco" which is Spanish or Portuguese for "secco" which is Italian for "sec."

SECT: English word having nothing to do with wine. Of course, there may be a group of religious fundamentalists out there that may have much to do with wine.

SEKT: German word having to do with wine. Actually, it refers to sparkling wines.

SEX: To some, the intended result of imbibing in wine.

SEMILLON: A thin skinned white grape used in the dessert wines of Sauternes as well as dry wines of Bordeaux. It is often blended with Sauvignon Blanc. Australia and other places blend it with Chardonnay. The thin skin makes it susceptible to "Noble Rot." Its thin skin probably also makes it susceptible to criticism.

SHERRY: When the crust is just right a slice of this pie can be very delicious. Oh wait, that's cherry. Sherry is actually a fortified wine from Jerez, Spain based on the Palomino or Pedro Ximenez grapes. That's all good and well as long as my cheeseburger isn't based on any Palomino.

SHIRAZ: As sure as Syrah is the main grape in France's Rhone Valley, this term refers to Syrah turned upside down, or rather down under. Australians just prefer the distinction of being distinct.

SOAVE: An Italian DOC. We don't mean like Doctor Guido, but rather Denominazione di Origine Controllata.

SOFT: A wine usually for early drinking due to low acidity and tannins. They don't mean that you should have it before noon.

SOMMELIER: These days one thinks of pirates from Somalia that know a lot about wine. It actually refers to a waiter who thinks he or she knows better than you what wine you should overpay for. Master Sommeliers were done away with by President Lincoln back in the 1863 harvest.

SOME LIAR: Your friend who just returned from a one day trip to Napa Valley and all of a sudden knows everything there is to know about wine.

SONOMA COUNTY: Northern California coastal county just west of Napa County that usually plays second fiddle to Napa. Many of the world's fine wines of different varietals are produced here. The two fiddles together play quite a tune.

SOUTH AFRICA: According to "Wikipedia" the online encyclopedia, this country is the world's eighth largest wine producer. Yes, most of their wines are white, but they've reformed some so let us celebrate that and move on.

SPAIN: Did you know that more wine is produced in the country of Spain than in the United States? Of course more Spanish is spoken in the cities of Los Angeles and Phoenix than in all of Spain. This is especially true at "Ross Dress for Less" stores on weekends.

SPARKLING WINE: That which many of the uninformed call Champagne. They're the same folks that call all cola beverages "Coke," all bandages "Band-Aids," all jeans "Levis," and all gypsum board "Sheetrock." All Champagne is sparkling wine, but not all sparkling wine is Champagne.

SPATLESE: This is a German term for a late harvest. The Germans used to be known for their punctuality.

SPICY: This word has generally the same meaning in wine as it does in food, movies, and language. Ay Caramba!

SPITTOON: Not the floor where this author grew up, but rather a receptacle for wine that is not swallowed during tasting. You could almost swear that some of this is repackaged and sold at a discount.

SPUMANTE: The Italian term for foaming or sparkling. An example of its use in a sentence could be "Hey mom, that Spumante dog just bit Timmy!"

SUGAR: That which converts to alcohol through fermentation.

SUGAR DADDY: That which converts an innocent young woman into a spoiled, greedy, insatiable beast of a person. This could be considered a form of fermentation as well.

SULFITES: The compound from sulfur dioxide that occurs in all wines and causes an allergic reaction in those sensitive to it. Although winemakers sometimes add sulfites to wine it is not to increase the reaction of those sensitive to it. That would be wrong.

SUPER TUSCAN: Either the Italian version of Clark Kent or the fine wines produced in Italy from Cabernet Sauvignon, Sangiovese and other grapes in varying blends.

SWEETNESS: Bringing flowers to Grandma. It is also one of the four basic tastes that we can identify. If you include umami then there are five basic tastes and you are soy up on things.

SYRAH: A red wine grape used in the production of rich tannic and spicy wines. It's called Shiraz in Australia and in the United States when reading an Australian wine label. The Rhône region is France produces great Syrah based wines like Chateauneuf Du Pape.

TABLE GRAPES: You can nail a bunch of these together to make a table; although it's been determined that wood works better. Some refer to table grapes as those for eating or juicing as opposed to winemaking.

TABLE WINE: Wine that tastes like a table…very woody. Generally, this refers to wines of lesser quality. In some blind tastings the table actually beat out the wine.

TAFELWEIN: Ever taste a German table? It can be wonderful if some sauerbraten has been spilt on it.

TANNIN: What some dads give to a child's hide even when it was his brother who broke the vase. Actually, it refers to the bit of tea like bitterness in wine that comes from the skins and seeds of grapes. Tannin is more pronounced in red wines and some of it goes away with aging. Dad's tannin went away with aging as well.

TART: The less than proper behavior of some female grapes. Needless to say it is a negative term in wine tasting caused by excessive acidity.

TARTARIC ACID: This is the acid that gives wine its tartness, duh. If balanced in a wine then good flavor and freshness comes through. It's when you have an imbalance that the tart gets too fresh.

TASTE: To each his own and to some none. If the subject was subjectivity then there could be no greater study material than wine. Oh yes, and food, and music, and movies, and art, and architecture, and cars and well you get the point.

TASTERY: A brand new term not yet accepted into the lexicon nor even seen in print or other use for that matter. It is a room or building or some such locale dedicated to sampling wine for the purpose of sampling wine. If you served pastries then it would be called a pastrytery. This might prove difficult to pronounce after a couple of cannoli.

TASTETOSTERONE: That mysterious hormone which enables one to taste over a dozen different wines in one sitting.

TASTEVIN: Wine's version of a computer geek's plastic pocket protector. It's that little metal tasting dish worn around the neck by some sommeliers. Please take it off before going into public.

TEMPRANILLO: This red wine grape in considered the best in Spain. It's called by other names depending on the part of Spain. Just as one might say Franco, another would say Frank and yet another would say Generalissimo.

TERROIR: French word meaning all aspects of a vineyard that affect a wine. These include climate, soil, sun, elevation, rain, fog, wind and the occasional poodle with bladder issues wandering the vineyards.

TERROR: The cost of a glass of wine in a San Francisco restaurant.

THOMPSON SEEDLESS: This is not a nickname for someone named Thompson whom happens to be sterile. It is those white, actually greenish, table grapes you see at the grocery store for eating and making raisins. Some winemakers like Gallo used Thompsons as a filler wine some time ago.

TIGNANELLO: Super Tuscan sounds better than Tignanello. This Sangiovese and Cabernet Sauvignon blend puts the super in the superb of those Tuscans.

TINTO: Not the Lone Ranger's sidekick, but rather his bottle of red wine as spoken in Spanish or Portuguese.

TOKAY: Hungry for some Hungarian dessert wine? Tokay is it. In Alsace, France the term is synonymous with Pinot Gris. Offering a glass of Tokay sounds more okay than a glass of grease (Gris).

TORRONTES: Argentina has been increasingly and successfully producing wine from this white grape. Some resemble a light Sauvignon Blanc. Others think it tastes like Muscat. It is hoped that they didn't mean Muskrat.

TREBBIANO: A French person would think that you were saying "very good" when in fact, you're just saying "mediocre white wine grape of Italy that is planted more than any other."

TROCKEN: This is the German word for dry. In America, some who prefer dry white wines have been heard to say "Keep on Trocken." You should stop serving those people.

TROCKENBEERENAUSLESE: Thankfully this isn't an acronym. The process for making these famous and expensive dessert wines is almost as painstaking as pronouncing it.

TUSCAN: An American style of interior and exterior décor originating in magazines and real estate brochures…not.

TUSCANY: If you want the real thing go here. Arguably, this is one of the most appealing wine growing areas that exist. This is especially true if you like sipping excellent wine such as some Super Tuscans, Chianti, Vino Nobile di Montepulciano, or Brunello di Montalcino in a setting of soft rolling hills, trees, wonderfully rustic architecture and just overall gorgeous setting.

UMBRIA: Tuscany's neighboring region to the east. It actually, sits smack in the middle of Italy and is home to Orvieto wine.

VARIETAL: This term refers to the grape from which a wine is made. Actually, they're made from a bunch of grapes since one grape would yield one drop of wine and think how small and difficult to open the bottles would be. Assuming that all or most of the grapes used are of the same variety such as Pinot Noir or Riesling, then the wine would be considered a varietal as opposed to a blend.

VAT: A large container used for storing wine. Some refer to that as a stomach or a bladder. Vats are also used to age wine and can be made of stainless steel, wood or even concrete.

VIN DE PAYS: French country wine made from grapes grown in a specific region. Not as low in quality as table wine since all of the grapes are somewhat related.

VIN DE TABLE: The lowest level of quality in French wine next to the spit bucket used at tastings. You can pretty much bet, however, that there are some gems to be found even in this classification.

VIN DE SCULLY: The best baseball announcer that there ever was.

VINO DE MESA: Mesa is Spanish for table and vino is Spanish for vin. This too refers to the lowest quality designation in terms of Spanish wine.

VINO NOBILE DE MONTEPULCIANO: A famous Sangiovese red wine from Tuscany. It could possibly be an opera as well.

VINTAGE: The year in which a wine was produced or harvested. They never begin a harvest on December 31st because if they can't finish before midnight, it messes with the vintage dating.

VIOGNIER: A white grape wine not commonly ordered in restaurants due to its pronunciation. You say "veeyonyea" and they bring you the Korean menu.

VITIS VINIFERA: The species of grape responsible for the great wines of the world.

VITO CORLEONE: One of the greatest film characters ever portrayed. Marlon Brando played this "godfather" in the movie whose title escapes me at the moment.

VOUVRAY: From this French Loire Valley appellation come white wines (Chenin Blanc) of fine quality. You can hear them sing at harvest time when famous actors come to visit…"Vouvray for Hollywood…"

WHATEVER: Rarely used wine tasting term for when the assessment of a wine is neither "yummy" nor "yucky."

WHITE PORT: The beverage of choice in South Central Los Angeles for those connoisseurs without employment. They were also known as winos or bums before the world became so politically correct. Nowadays they are called "self-sustaining urban ambassadors of oenology" or something like that. Coincidentally, there's a fortified white wine from Portugal that goes by the same name.

WHITE ZINFANDEL: Again, to be politically correct, this wine should be referred to as Anglo American Zinfandel but we'll keep it as Zin since it is not so thin skinned, nor is it white. This pink wine from the Zinfandel grape can be medium to sweet, refreshing and quite good.

WINE THIEF: You would think that this refers to a criminal running out of a liquor store without paying or perhaps even a restaurant charging $50 for a $10 bottle of wine. It is actually, a device used to take small amounts of wine from a cask or barrel for testing.

WINERY: The only gift better than wine would be one of these. This is where fruit becomes wine. It's a rotten place in the best possible sense of the word.

WHINERY: What the staff meetings where many work usually became.

WINE WINE SITUATION: This is when you have a bottle of white wine and a bottle of red wine both on the dinner table.

YEAST: The substance or organism from grape skins that is responsible for turning the sugar within the grape into alcohol. Of course, it is also used in making bread.

ZELL: If you've tasted a "Black Cat" German wine that was nothing special, it probably came from this village near the Mosel River. It may not be good but it zells.

ZINFANDEL: One of the great grape varieties thought to originate in Italy. The primitivo grape claims to be Zin's ancestor. This red grape makes fine wines in a variety of styles. The big booming bold ones can be zinfully good. Some producers of this wine use humorous, quirky, and catchy names such as "7 Deadly Zins," "Brazin," "Zynthesis," and the like. As if wine was something to joke about.

CHAPTER FIVE

RULES OF THUMB OR TIPS ON WINE

For starters don't use your thumb as a cork.

If over the age of 50 do not attempt to remove the cork from a bottle with your teeth.

When hosting a dinner party in which you're featuring a special wine, always make sure that you save the last bit for yourself.

If a fly lands in your wine observe it for a bit to make sure it's not too gross looking, then proceed to remove it before finishing your wine. Use a spoon to extract the insect as you wouldn't want to appear unsophisticated.

If the cork breaks off in the bottle while opening apply the number one rule of politics (blame someone else such as President George W. Bush).

If you break a glass while washing it at someone else's house use transparent tape to repair it. This may not work but it's worth a shot. Duct tape does not allow you to view the wine properly. How silly would that be?

While walking in a city park, if you happen upon a bottle of wine on the ground next to a less than sanitary gentleman apparently resting after a long day's work at the accounting firm and you're curious as to the wine's vintage, don't bother awakening the gentleman because that particular wine likely doesn't have a vintage.

You get what you pay for. An exception would be when you order a specific wine at a restaurant and the waiter, waitress, or trans server switches wines on you. This usually happens when they're out of what you ordered or if they've had a half bottle of something similar to your order sitting on the shelf somewhere.

You mistakenly purchased a bottle of the 2008 Cabernet for $4.99 and meant to purchase the 2007. Do you really think that it's worth wasting the $4.99 gallon of gasoline to make the exchange?

When toasting well into the evening with fine stemware be sure to pad your glass with some of that foam used to keep household pipes from freezing in winter. If not, you may need to refer to the tip about spilt wine.

Cheese softens the edges of tannins in wine; mainly cheap red wines. A tip for dinner party hosts could be to serve plenty of good cheese with your wine. A bad tip would be to recommend a block of Velveeta alongside a bottle of "Two Buck Chuck" when trying to impress Mr. Parker.

Sip; don't chug.

Use white wine to get a red wine spill out of the carpet. A dessert wine may work, but could also attract ants. In this case you'll require an anti-ant antidote. Another, albeit more expensive option for fixing the spill would be to spill a whole lot more red wine thus evening out the look. By the way, don't use red wine to clean a white wine spill.

Unlike a screw loose, a screw cap is not a bad thing. This is especially true when the wine in question costs more than $5.00. A bit of caution though; it can be a real pain in the **** removing the cork screw from the screw cap.

Wine tasting is not like golf. Warming up is not necessary and you don't really have to play 18 in one day to enjoy yourself.

Don't waste a fine wine on beer drinkers. If you went over to their place, you'd get a warm can of Bud Light while they enjoy the Samuel Adams thinking you none the wiser.

When asked your opinion of an expensive red wine and "yummy" or "yucky" won't quite cut the critique just mention a color, leather, and the word layers. The same rule applies if asked about the host's décor. If pressed further you may have to mention a fruit of some sort. As long as it isn't grapes you should be OK. If evaluating a white wine simply replace the word leather with vinyl.

When decanting a wine, the decanter should be larger than the bottle being poured.

Beware of hosts new to wine that just visited their first winery and bought an overpriced decanter complete with an aeration device. They may try to wow you with their new found knowledge. The old saying applies; "those who decant, teach." Maybe it's a new saying.

If the menu at a restaurant says red wine, white wine, and pink wine, it's perfectly acceptable to order a beer or tea.

When entering a tastery (a winery with a tasting room), if you trip at the front door, just turn around and leave. Why make matters worse? This rule applies even if it's the first winery of the day. You could try and salvage the visit by proclaiming "I'm not durnk," but who's going to believe you?

Some grocery stores have a sommelier or someone to assist you with a wine selection. If they ask if you prefer citrus, blackberries, ginger, or spice, you can ask them if they're sure that they're working in the right department of the grocery store. Of course, if you want to be sarcastic you could always say that you prefer the essence of pork roast and sauerkraut. That's why you're in the wine section. They'll leave you alone to browse. Seriously though, some of these folks can be very helpful. Just be aware of the upsell.

When opening a bottle for a tasting it is not necessary to tell everyone "stand back and give it some room to breathe." This isn't a sporting event. Of course, if someone brought a different wine, then it could become a sporting event.

When pouring a glass of wine, if it begins to flow over the sides of the glass, stop. Feel free to lap up any excess before serving.

The dashboard of your vehicle is not the ideal wine storage location. However, if you park your car in a wine cellar then this may be acceptable. In such a case be sure to place the bottles with the screw cap down in the cup holders. You don't want the screw cap to dry out.

Remember to wear a tastevin around your neck when you have company. It's one of those silver shallow cups that sommeliers use. You'll appear as cool as those guys with pocket protectors. If at some point during the evening you overhear the words "what an idiot," they're probably talking about someone else.

When a wine is described as "one for the masses" you can be pretty sure that if you serve it, the masses will revolt.

Wine that is alcohol free should be free. This bias extends to decaffeinated coffee, tofu burgers, soymilk, and BBQ chicken pizza.

A dry wine is good. A dry county is not.

Criticism is alright. Everyone's a critic. Just keep it in control or else a headline may one day read "Critically acclaimed Cribari critic in critical condition."

When the geography on a wine label reads California as in "California Merlot" and doesn't get more specific than that, the grapes could have come from anywhere in California. One person's pedigree is another's dog food.

Wine labels should not state "perfect for any occasion." Attending a DUI hearing, preschool, or meetings of Alcoholics Anonymous would not be appropriate wine occasions.

A wine described as super premium does not mean that it doubles as gasoline. In some cases it may not even be as palatable as gasoline. Please don't try this taste test.

Be skeptical of a wine described as engaging. Besides if the wine is in your mouth, then it could be said that you're probably more than just engaged.

Taste is subjective. Elect to be selective in your subjective suggestions.

You can look at your glass before tasting if you want. The only meaningful reason to do so would be bug identification. If there aren't any, then you're probably OK.

The "Old Vine" designation often seen on Zinfandel labels is subjective as well. Twenty years is not old if you're a person, but likely is if you're a grilled cheese sandwich.

At a wine tasting, before tasting and spitting the wine into a bucket, remember that there are thousands of thirsty sommeliers in India.

A tasting room is more important than a winery tour. You will know them by their fruit juice.

A wine that is made from grapes is organic enough for most folks.

Some wineries offer concerts, grape stomping, golfing, square dancing, and even weddings. Getting crushed and getting smashed shouldn't precede getting hitched. After the wedding there will always be plenty of time for golf. OK, maybe they don't offer square dancing.

A blind tasting does not mean that your specially trained dog does the tasting for you. If it did then they would serve the wine in toilets.

In describing a wine devoid of terroir you can say that "there is no there there."

Some people smash empty beer cans on their forehead. Don't try this with a wine bottle.

Some tasteries offer a private tour and tasting. This does not mean that you're left in a cold dark room to drink alone and find your own way.

Think outside the box wine.

"Less is more" does not apply to a wine glass.

APPENDIX

It appears that this book has had its appendix removed.

BIBLIOGRAPHY

MacNeil, Karen. The Wine Bible. New York, New York; Workman Publishing, 2001.

Williams-Sonoma. The Wine Guide. San Francisco, CA; Weldon Owen, Inc. and Williams- Sonoma, Inc. 1999

Oldman, Mark. Oldman's Guide to Outsmarting Wine. New York, NY; Penguin Group, 2004

Walton, Stuart. The World Encyclopedia of Wine. New York, NY; Smithmark Publishers. 1996

ABOUT THE AUTHOR

Greg A. Gonzalez was born in the South Central section of Los Angeles, California. Nowadays they don't even call it South Central. It's called something like "the South of LA" or maybe "Lower Los Angeles."

He spent many years as a civil servant serving civilly for the United States government.

Along the way he obtained a degree in Communication Studies from the prestigious California State University in Sacramento. There were a few other schools along the way such as Florence Avenue Elementary School.

Bouncing around California, Arizona, and Oregon he's managed to live a little in the wine country of Sonoma County. His knowledge of wine has been picked like grapes along the way.

Greg's been married to Christa, his wife and inspiration, for only 19 years. They live with Kujo in Northern California.

CPSIA information can be obtained at www.ICGtesting.com
Printed in the USA
LVOW04s0243241114

415273LV00014B/155/P

9 780983 425533